Marion Grussendorf

# Presenting in English

Sicher vortragen
Fragen souverän begegnen

POCKET BUSINESS TRAINING



Cornelsen

Dieses Buch enthält einige Auszüge aus dem Werk „Marion Grussendorf, English for Presentations“ (Short Course Series), die mit Erlaubnis des Cornelsen Verlags genutzt werden.

Verlagsredaktion: Elisabeth Dorner / Christine Schlagmann
Technische Umsetzung: Holger Stoldt, Düsseldorf
Grafiken: Roland Beier, Berlin
Umschlaggestaltung: Ellen Meister, Berlin
Titelfoto: © Hans Peter Merten / Getty Images

Informationen über Cornelsen Fachbücher und Zusatzangebote:
**www.cornelsen.de/berufskompetenz**

2. Auflage



Druck: Druckhaus Berlin-Mitte GmbH

ISBN 978-3-589-23888-0

Inhalt gedruckt auf säurefreiem Papier
aus nachhaltiger Forstwirtschaft.

# Vorwort

Präsentationen gehören heute für viele Menschen zum Berufsalltag. Egal, ob Sie Kunden ein neues Produkt vorstellen oder den eigenen Mitarbeitern die neue Firmenstrategie erläutern – Sie sollen einen Sachverhalt in interessanter und verständlicher Form vermitteln.

In der globalisierten Wirtschaftswelt kommt es immer häufiger vor, dass Sie dies nicht in der Muttersprache, sondern auf Englisch tun müssen. Das ist für viele eine enorme Hürde – schließlich verlassen sie das sichere sprachliche Umfeld und müssen sich neuen Herausforderungen stellen. Dabei tauchen zum Beispiel folgende Fragen auf:

- Bin ich sprachlich fit genug, um meine Präsentation auf dem gleichen Niveau zu halten wie in meiner Muttersprache?
- Bin ich darauf vorbereitet, dass ein internationales Publikum unter Umständen andere Erwartungen an mich hat als deutsche Zuhörer?

**Was erreichen Sie mit diesem Buch?**

Sie können sich mit diesem Buch gezielt auf eine Präsentation vorbereiten, indem Sie die für Ihre Zwecke passenden Satzbausteine auswählen und zusammenstellen. Die vielen Beispiele und Übungen helfen Ihnen, Ihre Kenntnisse rasch zu vertiefen. Außerdem erhalten Sie wertvolle Tipps zu den Fragen, was eine gelungene Präsentation ausmacht und welche Effekte und Ziele Sie mit bestimmten Mitteln erreichen können.

Sie erlangen mehr Sicherheit beim aktiven Einsatz grammatikalischer Formen, die Sie für Ihren Vortrag im Englischen brauchen.

Durch die Hinweise auf Besonderheiten im anglo-amerikanischen Präsentationsstil lernen Sie, sich auf ein internationales Publikum einzustellen und damit die Ziele, die Sie sich gesteckt haben, besser zu erreichen.

**Was Sie in diesem Buch finden:**

- Die wichtigsten englischen Wörter, Redewendungen und Satzbausteine für eine Präsentation
- Tipps zu Vorbereitung, Vorgehensweise und Gestaltung einer Präsentation
- Erläuterungen zu Unterschieden zwischen deutscher und internationaler Präsentationskultur
- Die wichtigsten Redewendungen im Überblick
- Übungen zu den einzelnen Kapiteln mit Lösungsvorschlägen
- Checkliste für englischsprachige Präsentationen

Köln, im Frühjahr 2009 *Marion Grussendorf*

# Inhalt

# 1 Vorbereitung und Einleitung

## 1.1 Konkrete Präsentationssituationen

**Sie begrüßen die Teilnehmer**

Wählen Sie eine Begrüßung, die dem Thema der Präsentation, der Situation und dem Publikum angemessen ist. Bedanken Sie sich dann für das Interesse bzw. die Anwesenheit Ihrer Zuhörer.

Eher formell:

- Good morning/afternoon, ladies and gentlemen. First of all, let me thank you all for coming here today.

Informell:

- Hello/Hi everyone. I'm happy that so many of you could make it today.

**Sie stellen sich vor**

Wenn Sie vor einem fremdem Publikum präsentieren oder Ihnen unbekannte Teilnehmer anwesend sind, stellen Sie sich mit Ihrem Namen, Titel und Ihrer Funktion in der Firma vor.

- Let me introduce myself. I'm Dave Elwood from …
- For those of you who don't know me, my name is Dave Elwood from …
- As you probably know, I'm the new HR manager.
- I'm head of logistics here at Air Spares.
- I'm here in my function as the Head of Logistics.

☞ **And by the way …:** *Aktuell* heißt im Englischen *current(ly)* oder *up-to-date* – nie ~~*actually*~~ (tatsächlich, eigentlich).

**Sie stellen Ihr Thema vor**

Verwenden Sie *topic* oder *subject,* um Ihr Thema vorzustellen:

- As you can see on the screen, our topic today is ...
- Today's topic is ...
- The subject of my presentation is ...

Oder wählen Sie eine allgemeinere Formulierung:

- What I'd like to present to you today is ...

**Sie beschreiben den Zweck Ihrer Präsentation**

Wenn Sie den Zweck bzw. das Ziel Ihrer Präsentation ausformulieren, verwenden Sie eine der folgenden Strukturen. Setzen Sie dabei verschiedene mögliche Strukturen ein, damit Ihr Vortrag auch sprachlich abwechslungsreich wird.

◆ *would like* + Infinitiv

- Today I'd like to tell you about our new plans.
- In particular, I'd like to show you how the market has developed since 2004.

◆ *going to* + Infinitiv

- This afternoon I'm going to report on the progress of our IT project.
- I'm going to describe the effects of globalisation on our business.

◆ *will* + Infinitiv

- I'll tell you about the new internet policy of our firm.
- I'll explain what this means for your workplace.

◆ *will be* + *-ing*-Form

- I'll be explaining the function of the new XB model.
- During the next 30 minutes we'll be looking at the changes in our online booking system.

Sie können auch Substantive wie *purpose, aim, objective* und *goal* verwenden, um eine Absicht auszudrücken:

- The purpose of my presentation is to ... (Zweck, Absicht)
- The aim of my presentation today is to ... (Ziel)
- The goals of my talk are ... (Ziele)
- Our objective is ... (Zielsetzung, Zweck)

**Sie erklären, für wen das Thema relevant ist**

Dabei empfiehlt es sich, statt *you* und *your* verstärkt Pronomen wie *we, us* oder *our* zu verwenden, die gemeinsames Interesse signalisieren:

- My talk is particularly relevant to those of us (you) who ...
- Today's topic is of particular interest to those of us (you) who ...
- My/The topic is very important for you because ...
- By the end of this talk we (you) will be familiar with ...

**Signposting: Die Struktur beschreiben**

Erklären Sie Ihrem Publikum, wie Ihre Präsentation aufgebaut ist, d.h., aus wie vielen Teilen sie besteht und wie genau die Reihenfolge der behandelten Punkte ist:

- I've divided my presentation into three (main) parts: ...
- In my presentation I'll focus on three major issues. First (of all), I'll be looking at ..., second ..., and third ...
- I'll begin / start off by explaining ...
- Then / Next / After that, I'll go on to ...
- Finally, I'll offer some solutions.

☞ **And by the way ...:** Wählen Sie bei Aufzählungen durchgängig die gleiche Form: *first, second, third* oder *firstly, secondly, thirdly.*

**Länge der Präsentation**

Sagen Sie Ihrem Publikum, wie lange die Präsentation dauern wird.

- My presentation will last/take about 20 minutes.
- It should take about 30 minutes to cover these issues.
- It will take about an hour to cover these points.

**Verteilen von Zusatzmaterial**

Wenn Sie Handouts wie Berichte, Statistiken, Grafiken etc. vorbereitet haben, sagen Sie, worum es sich dabei handelt und wann Sie das Material verteilen wollen. Dabei verwenden Sie einen der folgenden Sätze:

- Does everybody have a handout/brochure/report? Please take one and pass them on.
- Don't worry about taking notes. I've put all the important statistics on a handout for you.
- I'll be handing out copies of the PowerPoint slides at the end of my talk.

Oder Sie kündigen die spätere Übersendung von Material an:

- I'll e-mail the PowerPoint presentation to you.

**Wann können Fragen gestellt werden?**

Wenn Sie Fragen während der Präsentation zulassen möchten, sagen Sie:

- Feel free to ask questions at any time during my talk.
- If you have any questions, feel free to interrupt me at any time.

Wenn Sie Fragen nach Ihrer Präsentation beantworten möchten, sagen Sie:

- There will be time for questions after my presentation.

### Besondere Arten der Einleitung

Wenn Sie keine Standardeinleitung verwenden möchten, können Sie mit folgenden Strategien Ihre Präsentation beginnen:

**1. Frage**

- Is market research important for brand development?
- Do we really need quality assurance?

**2. Interessante/unbekannte Tatsache**

- According to an article I read recently, central banks are now buying euros instead of dollars.
- Did you know that fast food consumption has increased by 600 % in Europe since 2002?

**3. Anekdote**

- I remember when I attended a meeting in Paris. …
- At a conference in Madrid, I was once asked the following question: …

**4. Problemstellung**

- Suppose you wanted to set up a new call centre. How would you go about it?
- Imagine you had to reorganize the sales department. What would be your first step?

☞ **And by the way …:** Verwenden Sie immer ***at*** *the beginning* (nicht ~~*in*~~ *the beginning*), wenn Sie das deutsche *am Anfang von/des/der …* übersetzen wollen. Beispiel: *At the beginning of my talk, I am going to …*

## 1.2 Präsentationsstrategien und interkulturelle Aspekte

### Präsentieren in der Fremdsprache

Das Präsentieren vor Publikum ist keine leichte Aufgabe, in der Fremdsprache wird es jedoch zur echten Herausforderung. Bei einer nicht besonders gelungenen Präsentation vermutet man oft, dass sprachliche Defizite der Grund sind. Das ist aber meist gar nicht der Fall.

> Wenn Sie Ihren Stoff inhaltlich beherrschen und einige grundsätzliche Strategien beherzigen, können Sie als Nicht-Muttersprachler sogar Pluspunkte sammeln.

Schließlich ist ein Vortrag in einer Fremdsprache eine besondere Leistung, die Ihr Publikum honoriert. Sprachliche Fehler wird man Ihnen gerne verzeihen, solange Ihr Vortrag interessant ist und dem Zuhörer Nutzen bringt.

### Vorbereitung – der Schlüssel zum Erfolg

Vielleicht gibt es geborene Präsentationstalente, aber die meisten von uns müssen sich eine gute Präsentation erarbeiten. Auf keinen Fall sollten Sie sich auf spontane Eingebungen und Kreativität verlassen, denn der Schlüssel zum Erfolg einer Präsentation ist immer die gründliche Vorbereitung.

Planen Sie im Vorfeld genau, was Sie für wen präsentieren und wie Sie Ihr Thema vortragen wollen. Denken Sie dabei auch an den Zeitfaktor, d.h., probieren Sie aus, wie lange Ihr Vortrag dauert und ob er in den gesteckten Zeitrahmen passt.

Gehen Sie die einzelnen Punkte immer wieder durch, bis Sie jeden Satz verinnerlicht haben.

Üben Sie die englischen Sätze und Redewendungen, die für Ihren Vortrag wichtig sind. Sprechen Sie laut vor sich hin – wenn möglich, nehmen Sie sich selbst auf, um sich später überprüfen zu können.

**Umgang mit Nervosität**

Ein paar nützliche Grundregeln:

**1. Bereiten Sie sich vor.**
Nichts ist so beruhigend wie eine gute Vorbereitung. Wenn Sie sich mit dem Thema ausführlich beschäftigt haben, bringt Sie so leicht nichts aus der Ruhe.

**2. Entspannen Sie sich.**
Atem- und Dehnübungen können helfen, innere Anspannung zu lösen.

**3. Machen Sie sich mit Raum und Geräten vertraut.**
Sehen Sie sich vor der Präsentation die Räumlichkeiten an und stellen Sie sicher, dass alle benötigten Geräte vorhanden sind und funktionieren.

**4. Konzentrieren Sie sich auf Ihr Thema.**
Richten Sie Ihre ganze Aufmerksamkeit auf Ihre Aussagen und Ziele – nicht auf Ihre Ängste.

**5. Malen Sie sich Ihren Erfolg aus.**
Stellen Sie sich vor, wie Sie laut und deutlich sprechen. Dann stellen Sie sich vor, dass Ihnen das Publikum laut applaudiert.

**Aufbau einer Präsentation**

Wie im Deutschen bestehen englischsprachige Präsentationen in der Regel aus drei Teilen:

1. Einführung/Einleitung
2. Hauptteil
3. Schluss

Manchmal findet man noch einen vierten Teil, der im Englischen als *call for action* bezeichnet wird. Darin werden die Teilnehmer aufgefordert, etwas in die Praxis umzusetzen, was ihnen während der Präsentation vorgestellt wurde.

**Techniken, um die Aufmerksamkeit zu wecken**

Um die Aufmerksamkeit der Zuhörer zu wecken, können Sie für den Anfang Ihrer Präsentation eine der folgenden Techniken wählen.

### ☑ Sie stellen eine (rhetorische) Frage

So beziehen Sie Ihre Zuhörer in das Thema ein und veranlassen sie, sich Gedanken über eine Antwort zu machen.

- Do we need to improve customer service?

### ☑ Sie beginnen mit einer interessanten Tatsache

Sie haben von einem ungewöhnlichen Ereignis oder einer bemerkenswerten Tatsache gehört oder darüber gelesen und nehmen dies als Aufhänger für Ihr Thema.

- Did you know that computer giant Dell plans to double its workforce in India?

### ☑ Sie beginnen mit einer Geschichte

Sie schildern eine Begebenheit aus Ihrem Erfahrungsbereich, die für Ihr Thema oder Ihre Absicht relevant ist. Diese Geschichte erzählen Sie aber nicht zu Ende, sondern brechen sie vor der Auflösung ab. Damit schaffen Sie bis zur Klärung im Schlussteil einen Spannungsbogen.

- At a conference in Leeds, I was once asked the following question: ...

### ☑ Sie konfrontieren die Zuhörer mit einem Problem

Sie können Ihr Publikum gezielt aktivieren, wenn Sie es mit einem konkreten Problem konfrontieren, das gelöst werden soll. Die Zuhörer sind so gefordert, sich selbst mit dem Thema auseinanderzusetzen statt nur zuzuhören.

- Suppose you wanted to sell this technology in China. How would you go about it?

**Tipps für die Einleitung: Wesentliche Elemente und ihre Funktion**

**1. Sich vorstellen**
Den ersten Teil der Präsentation nutzen Sie, um sich dem Publikum vorzustellen und es mit Thema und Zielsetzung vertraut zu machen.

**2. Beziehung zum Publikum schaffen**
Sie bauen im ersten Teil Ihrer Präsentation eine Beziehung zu Ihren Zuhörern auf – im Englischen *rapport* genannt –, die den Erfolg Ihrer Präsentation entscheidend beeinflussen wird.

**3. Zuhörer motivieren**
Experten sind sich einig, dass die ersten paar Minuten darüber entscheiden, mit welchen Erwartungen und welchem Interesse das Publikum Ihren Ausführungen folgen wird.
Verschwenden Sie diese wertvolle Zeit deshalb nicht mit langweiligen Phrasen, sondern machen Sie sich Gedanken, wie Sie Ihre Zuhörer für sich und Ihr Thema gewinnen können.

**4. Den Fahrplan vorgeben: Signposting**
Geben Sie eine kurze und einfache Übersicht über die Struktur und den Ablauf Ihres Vortrags – ein sehr wichtiges Element bei Präsentationen vor angloamerikanischem Publikum (mehr dazu auf S. 54).

**5. Nervosität überwinden**
Nutzen Sie die Einleitung, um anfängliche Nervosität abzubauen und an Sicherheit zu gewinnen. Je besser die Vorbereitung ist, desto leichter gelingt dies.

☞ **And by the way ...:** Verwechseln Sie nicht *to deal with* (sich kümmern um, handeln von) mit *to deal in* (handeln mit).

**Signposting: Gezielt durch den Vortrag führen**

Wird der Begriff Signposting (Wegweiser) im Zusammenhang mit Präsentationen benutzt, so ist damit eine gängige Methode der Strukturierung gemeint.

Dabei stellt man sich Folgendes vor: Die Präsentation ist eine Reise, bei der die Zuhörer zu einem bestimmten Ziel geführt werden sollen. Damit sie auch tatsächlich dort ankommen, benötigen sie klar verständliche und präzise Wegweiser. Anders gesagt:

> Signposting bedeutet, dass Sie Ihrem Publikum am Anfang des Vortrags mitteilen, wohin die Reise geht und wie Sie das Ziel erreichen wollen.

Sie sagen beispielsweise, welche Punkte Sie behandeln, in welcher Reihenfolge und zu welchem Zweck.

Signposting bedeutet auch, dass Sie Ihre Zuhörer im Verlauf einer Präsentation immer wieder mitnehmen, d.h., sie kurz daran erinnern, wo genau sie sich jetzt gerade befinden und wie es anschließend weitergeht.

Bei Präsentationen in der angloamerikanischen Geschäftswelt ist diese Signposting-Methode so weit verbreitet, dass sie als gängiger Standard gilt.
Deutsche Muttersprachler scheuen oft vor diesen wiederkehrenden Wegweisern zurück – aus Angst, das Publikum könnte dies als plump oder lehrerhaft empfinden.

Der Grund für Missverständnisse liegt hier vor allem in einer unterschiedlichen Erwartungshaltung:

- Das angloamerikanische Publikum erwartet einfache und klare Strukturen, um sich auf die Kernaussagen konzentrieren zu können.
- Ein deutsches Publikum könnte dieses Signposting eher als Missachtung der eigenen intellektuellen Fähigkeiten empfinden und sich unterfordert fühlen.

**Amerikanische und deutsche Präsentationen im Vergleich**

Da Präsentationen von vielen Faktoren geprägt werden, ist es nicht möglich, für jedes Land eine typische und verbindliche Präsentationskultur zu beschreiben.
Ein Vergleich zwischen amerikanischer und deutscher Präsentationsweise legt aber die Vermutung nahe, dass folgende Aspekte im amerikanischen Umfeld anders bewertet und gehandhabt werden:

☑ **Stärkere Rolle des Präsentierenden**

Der Präsentierende nimmt oft eine sehr aktive Rolle ein und sieht sich selbst als Gestalter und Unterhalter – persönlich verantwortlich für den Erfolg der Präsentation. Dazu gehören Körpersprache und der Einsatz der eigenen Persönlichkeit. Deshalb präsentieren Amerikaner ihr Thema häufig mit großem Enthusiasmus und viel Engagement. In deutschsprachigen Präsentationen steht oft das Thema im Vordergrund – der Präsentierende nimmt sich als Person zurück.

☑ **Mehr Interaktion mit dem Publikum**

Die Teilnehmer sehen sich als Individuen und möchten mit ihren persönlichen Wünschen und Erwartungen wahrgenommen werden. Für den Vortragenden bedeutet das:

> Geben Sie den Zuhörern immer wieder zu erkennen, dass Sie sich mit ihren verschiedenen Bedürfnissen beschäftigt haben.

Hilfreich ist auch, wenn Sie öfter einfließen lassen, welche Punkte für welche Teilnehmer besonders relevant sind.

☑ **Motivation der Teilnehmer**

Oft dienen Präsentationen vor amerikanischem Publikum vor allem dazu zu motivieren, zu begeistern oder auf ein Thema positiv einzustimmen. Deutschsprachige Präsentationen zielen oft mehr auf die Vermittlung von Fakten und Wissen und werden daher viel sachlicher vorgetragen.

## 1.3 Vokabeln und Redewendungen auf einen Blick

### Die Teilnehmer begrüßen

- Good morning/afternoon, ladies and gentlemen.
- Hello/Hi everyone.
- First of all, let me thank you all for coming here today.
- I'm happy/delighted that so many of you could make it today.

### Sich vorstellen

- Let me introduce myself. I'm David Barnes from …
- For those of you who don't know me, my name is …
- As you probably know, I'm the new sales manager.
- I'm head of HR here at Altec.
- I'm here in my function as the Head of Controlling.

### Das Thema vorstellen

- As you can see on the screen, our topic today is …
- Today's topic is …
- What I'd like to present to you today is …
- The subject of my presentation is …

### Zielsetzung erklären

- This morning I'd like to bring you up-to-date on our department.
- I'm going to report on the new division.
- I'll begin by explaining the function.
- After that, I'll move on to my next point.
- I'll be talking about our guidelines for Internet use.

**Zielgruppe**

- My talk is particularly relevant to those of you/us who …
- Today's topic is of particular interest to those of you/us who are involved in …
- My/The topic is very important for you because …
- By the end of this talk you will be familiar with …

**Struktur erklären**

- I've divided my presentation into three (main) parts: x, y and z.
- In my presentation I'll focus on three major issues.
- First (of all), I'll be looking at …, second …, and third …
- I'll begin / start off by explaining … Then / Next / After that, I'll go on to … Finally, I'll offer some solutions.

**Zeitlicher Rahmen**

- My presentation will last about 20 minutes.
- It should take about 30 minutes to cover these issues.

**Zusatzmaterial verteilen**

- Does everybody have a handout/brochure/report? Please take one, and pass them on.
- Don't worry about taking notes. I've put all the important facts/statistics/graphics on a handout for you.
- I'll be handing out copies of the PowerPoint slides at the end of my talk.
- I'll e-mail the PowerPoint presentation to you.

**Fragen**

- There will be time for questions after my presentation.
- If you have any questions, feel free to interrupt me at any time.
- Feel free to ask questions at any time during my talk.

**Aufmerksamkeit der Teilnehmer wecken durch …**

**… eine (rhetorische) Frage**

- Is this development important for our market position?
- Do we really need better customer service?

**… interessante Fakten**

- According to an article I read recently, property prices have risen by 250% in London since the mid 80s.
- Did you know that coffee is good for your health?

**… eine Geschichte**

- I remember when I attended a meeting in Paris. …
- At a conference in Madrid, I was once asked the following question: …

**… ein Problem**

- Suppose you wanted to break into the Chinese market. How would you go about it?
- Imagine you had to increase output in the claims department. What would be your first step?

## 1.4 Übungen

### Ü1 Setzen Sie das passende Wort ein.

**Presentation 1**

present – first of all – glad – thank – particularly – introduce

1. ________________ , let me ___________ you all for being here today.
2. I'm ___________ that so many of you could come.
3. Let me ________________ myself. My name is Jochen Rücker.
4. I'm here today to ________________ our new semi-automatic shelving system.
5. My talk is ________________ relevant to those of you who place orders for the different parts we supply.

**Presentation 2**

involved – screen – important – make – notice – topic – happy

6. I'm ___________ that so many of you could ______________ it today at such short _____________.
7. As you can see on the ______________, our ______________ today is project documentation.
8. This is extremely ________________ for all of us who are directly ______________ in international project management, right?

**Ü2 Vervollständigen Sie die Sätze mit der richtigen Form des Verbs in Klammern und einem der Satzenden.**

a you on the proposed training project.
b you up to date on SEKO's investment plans.
c about EU tax reform.
~~d you how the database works.~~
e you an overview of our present market position.
f by telling you about what Jane's group is working on.
g at business opportunities in Asia.
h on our financial targets for the division.

**Beispiel:**
1 (show): I'll be
~ I'll be showing you how the database works.

2 (give): Today I'd like to ______________________________

3 (talk): During the next two hours we'll be ______________________________

4 (bring): I'd like to ______________________________

5 (report): This afternoon I'm going to ______________________________

6 (update): Today I'd like to ______________________________

7 (look): This morning we'll be ______________________________

8 (begin): Today I'll ______________________________

**Ü3 Setzen Sie den passenden Ausdruck ein.**

**Presentation 1**

concept for – I'd like to present – today's topic – I'm the new – to come here – I'll need your help – I'm aware that – as you probably

Good afternoon. _______________ ❶ you all have very tight schedules, so I appreciate you taking the time _______________ ❷ today.
_______________ ❸ know, my name is Susan Webster. _______________ ❹ human resources manager here at Weston Ltd. What _______________ ❺ to you today is my department's new _______________ ❻ improving our in-company training and qualification programmes. This is based on feedback from your departments.
_______________ ❼ will be very important for you as department heads, since _______________ ❽ to evaluate and select candidates for training.

**Ü4 Ergänzen Sie die Einleitungen mit den passenden Wörtern.**

responsible – came across – imagine – asking you – tell you why – go about it – you know – magazines – did you know

1. _______________ , I was sitting in the waiting room at the dentist's the other day and I _______________ something very interesting in one of the _______________ that was lying there.

2. _______________ you worked in a small to medium-sized company and were _______________ for making people in your company aware of health and safety issues. How would you _______________ ?

3. ____________________ that the number of possible ways of playing the first four moves per side in a game of chess is 318,979,564,000?

4. So, let me start by ____________ a question. Why should we introduce a double quality check here at Auto Spares & Parts? Well, I'm here today to ____________________ .

**Ü5 Ordnen Sie einen förmlichen Satz jeweils einem weniger förmlichen zu.**

| | | |
|---|---|---|
| 1. Good afternoon, ladies and gentlemen. | a What I want to do today is ... | ☐ |
| 2. Today I would like to ... | b I know you are all very busy ... | ☐ |
| 3. Let me just start by introducing myself. My name is ... | c As you know, I'm ... | ☐ |
| 4. It's a pleasure to welcome you today. | d OK, shall we get started? | ☐ |
| 5. In my presentation I would like to report on ... | e It's good to see you all here. | ☐ |
| 6. The topic of today's presentation is ... | f Hi, everyone. | ☐ |
| 7. I suggest that we begin now. | g Today I'm going to talk about ... | ☐ |
| 8. I'm aware that you all have very tight schedules ... | h In my talk I'll tell you about ... | ☐ |

**Ü6 Setzen Sie die richtige Präposition ein.**

about – at – during – for – into – of – on – to – with

1. Thank you ________ coming all this way.
2. I've divided my presentation ________ three parts.
3. First of all, I'll give you an overview ________ our financial situation.
4. First, we'll be looking ________ the company's sales in the last two quarters.
5. In the first part of my presentation I'll focus ________ the current project status.
6. Point one deals ________ APG's new regulations for Internet use.
7. Secondly, I'll talk ________ our investment in office technology.
8. After that I'll move on ________ the next point.
9. ________ the next 20 minutes, we'll be dealing with software problems and how to solve them.

**Ü7 Setzen Sie die Satzteile richtig zusammen.**

| | |
|---|---|
| 1. For those of you who don't know me, ... | a to take notes. Everything is on the handout. ☐ |
| 2. Feel free to ... | b how the system works. ☐ |
| 3. This won't take more ... | c I'm Bob Kay in charge of the software division. ☐ |
| 4. I'll be passing out ... | d ask questions at any time. ☐ |
| 5. This part of the presentation will take ... | e for questions after my talk. ☐ |
| 6. I'll start off by giving you ... | f an overview of our product range. ☐ |
| 7. There's no need .... | g handouts in a few minutes. ☐ |
| 8. There will be time ... | h than 20 minutes of your time. ☐ |
| 9. After that, I'm going to explain ... | i about 10 minutes. ☐ |

## Fit for Presenting in English?
## Test Yourself!

**T1 Bringen Sie die Sätze in die richtige Reihenfolge.**

a I've divided my talk into three main parts.
b The topic of my presentation today is …
c As you probably know, my name is…
d This will be particularly relevant to those of us who …
e There will be time for questions after my presentation.
f My presentation will take about 45 minutes.
g I'm happy that so many of you could make it here today.
h I'll be handing out copies at the end of my talk.

1. ______________________________

2. ______________________________

3. ______________________________

4. ______________________________

5. ______________________________

6. ______________________________

7. ______________________________

8. ______________________________

**T2 Bilden Sie vollständige Sätze. Benutzen Sie für jeden Satz jede Spalte.**

| | | |
|---|---|---|
| 1 Did you know that | compete with the Chinese? | I tend to agree with that! |
| 2 I read in an article | you won a million euros. | by eliminating one olive from each salad served in first class? |
| 3 Imagine | that overweight in the US is far more dangerous than terrorism. | Who would you tell first? |
| 4 Can we really | AA saved $40,000 | Of course we can! |

**T3 Übersetzen Sie die folgenden Sätze.**

1. Gut, lassen Sie uns anfangen.
2. Das Thema meiner heutigen Präsentation ist Kundenzufriedenheit.
3. Meine Präsentation wird etwa eine halbe Stunde dauern.
4. Ich konzentriere mich auf drei Punkte.
5. Als Erstes werden wir uns den aktuellen Projektstatus ansehen.
6. Wussten Sie, dass dieses Auto in China sehr beliebt ist?

**T4 Setzen Sie das passende Wort ein.**

after – all – areas – divided – finally – start – then – third

**A**

I'll be talking to you today about the after-sales service plans we offer. I'll ________________ (1) by describing the various packages in detail. ________________ (2) I'll go on to show you some case studies. ________________ (3), I'll discuss how you can choose the best plan to meet your customers' needs.

**B**

I've ________________ (4) my talk into three main parts. First of ________________ (5), I'll tell you something about the history of our company. ________________ (6) that I'll describe how the company is structured and finally, I'll give you some details about our range of products and services.

**C**

I'd like to update you on what we've been working on over the last year. I'll focus on three main ________________ (7): first, our joint venture in Asia; second, the new plant in Charleston. And ________________ (8), our redevelopment project.

**T5 Ersetzen Sie die fett gedruckten Ausdrücke durch passende Wörter aus der Liste.**

after that – begin – I'm – realize – responsible for – sections – turn

1. I'll **start off** by showing you the main functions.

   ______________________________

2. I've divided my presentation into three **parts**.

   ______________________________

3. For those of you who don't know me, **my name is** Gordon Smith.

   ______________________________

4. **Then** I'll **move on** to the problems.

   ______________________________

5. I'm the project manager **in charge of** our Dubai building project.

   ______________________________

6. **I'm aware** that you're all busy preparing for the annual meeting.

   ______________________________

# 2 Medien bewusst einsetzen

## 2.1 Konkrete Präsentationssituationen

**Medien ankündigen und darauf verweisen**
Erklären Sie dem Publikum, welche Präsentationsmedien und Visualisierungsmittel eingesetzt werden.

- In my presentation I'll be using PowerPoint slides (Präsentationsfolien).
- I'm going to show you a short promotional video.
- In my talk I will mainly rely on statistics.

Während der Präsentation kündigen Sie immer an, was Sie als Nächstes zeigen möchten:

- The next chart will show ...
- Now I'd like to show you ...
- You will now see ...
- I have a slide here that shows ...

Wenn Sie auf etwas verweisen wollen, ohne konkrete Medien oder Visualierungsmittel zu nennen, können Sie allgemeine Formulierungen wie *As you can see* ... oder *Here we/you can see* ... wählen.

- As you can see here, our sales have doubled.
- Here we can see the latest figures.

Wollen Sie ein Visualisierungsmittel nennen, achten Sie unbedingt auch auf die Präpositionen.

- As you can see **on** the flipchart / screen (Bildschirm) / slide (Folie, Dia) ...
- As you can see **from** the picture / graph (Kurve) / table (Tabelle, Tafel) ...

Sehr gebräuchlich sind Ausdrücke mit *look,* wenn man das Publikum auf etwas aufmerksam machen will.

- Let's now look at the figures.
- Please take a look at these findings.
- Let's have a look at this graph.

Oft ist es günstig, dies gleich mit einem erklärenden Satz zu verbinden.

- Let's have a look at this graph which shows ...
- Take a look at this graph which illustrates ...

Andere Möglichkeiten:

- According to this bar chart (Säulendiagramm), our net profit has doubled.
- The problem is illustrated in the next pie chart (Tortendiagramm).
- To illustrate this, let's have a closer look at ...

### Abbildungen erklären

Bei komplizierten Grafiken sind oft Erklärungen notwendig. Kündigen Sie eine kurze Erläuterung an.

- First, let me quickly explain …

Erklären Sie, wo die wesentlichen Elemente zu sehen sind.

- You can see that the new models are listed at the top / at the bottom.
- In the left-hand corner you will see …
- The red line gives us …
- The green line here shows …
- The figures in the first row (Reihe) indicate …
- What you can see across the bottom is …
- If you look at the column on the left, you can see …
- The key on the left shows you which colour represents which area.

### Auf wichtige Punkte hinweisen

Weisen Sie auf Punkte, Fakten und Entwicklungen hin, die in Ihrer Grafik von Bedeutung sind.

- Let's take a closer look at …
- Let's look more closely at …
- I'd like to point out here that …
- What I'd like to focus on here is …
- Let me draw your attention to …

### Trends in Diagrammen oder Kurven beschreiben

Im Englischen gibt es etliche Ausdrücke, mit denen man Trends beschreiben kann. Eine kleine Auswahl zeigt die Übersicht auf der folgenden Seite.
Wenn Sie ausdrücken möchten, um wie viel etwas wächst oder fällt, verwenden Sie ein entsprechendes Verb und *by:*

- Our export business has grown **by** 20%.

### Trends beschreiben

**Tendenz steigend**

- *to climb* (steigen, klettern)
- *to expand* (expandieren)
- *to grow* (wachsen)
- *to rise, increase* (steigen)

Beispiele:

- In April the rate of unemployment rose to 5 million.
- The US economy has grown rapidly over the past four months.

**Tendenz fallend**

- *to decline* (sinken, zurückgehen)
- *to decrease* (abnehmen, fallen)
- *to drop, fall* (fallen)

Beispiele:

- The number of German investors has dropped.
- Our export business declined by 10 % last year.

**Weitere Ausdrücke**

- *to fluctuate* (schwanken)
- *to hit a low* (einen Tiefpunkt erreichen)
- *to reach a high* (einen Höhepunkt erreichen)
- *to remain stable* (stabil bleiben)

Beispiele:

- After the oil crisis petrol prices reached a high in May.
- The number of customers has remained stable.

Auf welchen Stand etwas wächst oder fällt, drückt man mit dem Verb und *to* aus:

- The number of passengers rose **to** 500,000.

## Zahlen vereinfachen

Oft ist es sinnvoll, komplizierte Zahlen zu vereinfachen, indem man sie auf ganze Zahlen auf- oder abrundet. Hier einige Beispiele:

- Etwa, ungefähr

  - We spent **about** €20,000 on new software.
  - The cost will be **around** 2 million.
  - It will take **approximately** one year to complete it.
  - **Roughly** 10% of our staff agree.

- (Etwas) mehr

  - This is **a little more than** what we earned in 2006.
  - Last month we had **just over** 12,000 members.
  - **Well over** 60% of our products went to Spain.

- (Etwas) weniger

  - Our market share was **a little less than** 4%.
  - We sold **just under** 1 million articles.
  - The figure is **nearly** the same as last year's figure.
  - The distance is **almost** 6,500 km.

## Entwicklungen präzise beschreiben

Um Entwicklungen präzise zu beschreiben, gibt es folgende Möglichkeiten:

- Verb mit Adverb

  - Over the past two years the number **has dropped significantly.**
  - Sales **increased slightly** in summer.

- Substantiv mit Adjektiv

  In diesem Fall benötigen Sie einleitende Wörter wie beispielsweise *there was / has been, we see, we have seen, we notice* etc.

  - There was a **sudden increase** in prices.
  - In August, we notice a **moderate fall.**

## 2.2 Präsentationsstrategien und interkulturelle Aspekte

Beachten Sie zunächst zwei wichtige Grundregeln:

☑ **Visuelle Elemente sind Unterstützung!**
Denken Sie bei der Auswahl und Gestaltung von Präsentationsmedien immer daran, dass diese Ihren Vortrag unterstützen, nicht davon ablenken sollen.
Bereiten Sie jedes visuelle Element einzeln und sorgfältig vor und überprüfen Sie kritisch, ob es diesen Zweck erfüllt.

☑ **Weniger ist oft mehr!**
Die Kunst des Präsentierens besteht auch darin, dem Zuhörer das Wesentliche zu vermitteln. Ihre Aufgabe ist es, im Vorfeld eine sinnvolle Auswahl zu treffen.

### Bildmaterial richtig auswählen, aufbereiten und einsetzen

☑ **Anzahl der Folien beschränken**
Egal, wie gelungen Ihre Folien sind und wie wichtig der Inhalt sein mag – Ihr Publikum ist ab einer gewissen Anzahl überfordert. Eine Folie pro Minute ist das Maximum.

☑ **PowerPoint-Effekte sinnvoll nutzen**
Wenn im angloamerikanischen Raum von „Death by PowerPoint" die Rede ist, dann ist damit die übertriebene Verwendung von Effekten und deren Wirkung auf das Publikum gemeint.
PowerPoint bietet vielfältige und interessante Möglichkeiten, eine Präsentation zu gestalten. Das sollte Sie aber nicht dazu verführen, sie tatsächlich alle zu nutzen. Verwenden Sie Textanimationen, Soundeffekte, farbigen Bildschirmhintergrund und Flash-Überleitungen nur sparsam – wenn überhaupt.

☑ **Text**
Verwenden Sie möglichst wenig Text – gerade so viel wie nötig, um Ihre Aussagen zu unterstützen.

☑ **Interesse wecken (Media Teasing)**
Die im englischsprachigen Raum als „Media Teasing" bezeichnete Methode bedeutet, dass Sie das Publikum durch gezielte Ankündigungen vorbereiten und gleichzeitig die Neugierde auf die nun folgenden visuellen Medien wecken.

☑ **Zeit zum Erfassen der Grafik etc.**
Bevor Sie zu sprechen beginnen, lassen Sie den Teilnehmern etwas Zeit, um das Gezeigte zu erfassen.

☑ **TTT: touch – turn – talk**
Deuten Sie auf (oder berühren Sie) das, was Sie beschreiben, drehen Sie sich zum Publikum und sprechen Sie dann.

☑ **Wallpaper**
Wenn Sie gerade nicht über eine Folie, Grafik etc. sprechen, sollte sie auch für die Teilnehmer nicht sichtbar sein (Ablenkungsgefahr). Bei einer PowerPoint-Präsentation kehren Sie zum schwarzen Bildschirm zurück oder verwenden Sie eine Art Wallpaper – z.B. ein Firmenlogo.

☑ **Nicht vorlesen**
Lesen Sie nicht einfach wörtlich von der Folie ab – heben Sie Wichtiges besonders hervor.

☑ **Interpretieren Sie das Gezeigte**
Die Teilnehmer wollen wissen, was sie sehen und warum sie es gezeigt bekommen. Erklären Sie also stets, was eine Grafik bedeutet oder welche Schlüsse sich daraus ziehen lassen.

> ☞ **And by the way …:** Verwechseln Sie nicht *because* (weil) mit *because of* (wegen).

## Tipps für die Gestaltung von Folien

**Rule of six (oder: six by six guideline)**
Vor allem in der angloamerikanischen Präsentationskultur ist die „Rule of six“ eine gängige Regel. Sie besagt: maximal sechs Wörter pro Zeile, maximal sechs Zeilen pro Folie!

**Überschrift**
Entwerfen Sie aussagekräftige Überschriften, die den Inhalt der Folie präzise und knapp umreißen.

**Bullet points**
Fassen Sie Ihre Kernideen in wenige Worte – bilden Sie keine ganzen Sätze. Seien Sie dabei konsequent, d.h. zum Beispiel: Verwenden Sie in allen *bullet points* die gleiche Zeit, die gleiche Struktur (am besten Verb vorne, Groß- oder Kleinbuchstaben am Anfang).

**Gute Lesbarkeit**
Wählen Sie eine gut lesbare Schriftgröße (z.B. 24 Punkt). Bevorzugen Sie Schriften ohne „Schnörkel“. Farben sollten Sie sparsam einsetzen, da mehrere Farben oft verwirren.

**Text und Grafik**
Mischen Sie wenn möglich Text und Grafik bei der Gestaltung von Folien, und zwar nach dem Motto: Ein Bild sagt mehr als tausend Worte. Möglicherweise haben Sie die Erfahrung bereits selbst gemacht: Text allein ist auf die Dauer langweilig und ermüdend.

### ☑ Abwechslungsreiche Sprache

Wenn Sie Folien, Grafiken etc. erklären, wechseln Sie im Ausdruck ab, d.h. verwenden Sie immer wieder andere Formulierungen, auch wenn Sie ähnliche oder dieselben Sachverhalte beschreiben.

## Sprachliche Aspekte beim Umgang mit Medien

### ☑ Trends beschreiben: welche Zeitform?

Wenn Sie Entwicklungen erklären, müssen Sie zwischen mehreren Zeitformen auswählen. Ganz wichtig ist dabei die Unterscheidung zwischen der Vergangenheit (*Past Tense: went, did*) und dem Perfekt (*Present Perfect: have gone, has done*). Beachten Sie die folgende Regel:

- *Past Tense*

  Sie beschreiben eine Entwicklung in der Vergangenheit, die zu einem bestimmten Zeitpunkt (oder Zeitraum) stattfand und abgeschlossen ist.

  Signalwörter: *last* year, *in* 2005, two years *ago*.

  – Sales **rose** by 30 % last year.

- *Present Perfect*

  Sie beschreiben einen Trend, der in der Vergangenheit begonnen hat und noch andauert.

  Signalwörter: *for* 10 years, *since* 2001, *this* year, *in the past few* years.

  Beachten Sie: *since* bei Zeitpunkten, *for* bei Zeitspannen.

  – Sales **have risen** since 2005.

Nehmen Sie niemals deutsche Sätze als Vorlage, da die deutschen Zeiten meist nicht den englischen entsprechen:

– Letztes Jahr **haben** wir die Auftragsmenge **gesteigert.** *(Perfekt)*
– Last year we **increased** the order volume. (*Past Tense*)

### ☑ Aussagen verstärken

Sie können Ihre Aussage verstärken, wenn Sie Adjektive und Adverbien einsetzen. Es gibt diese drei Möglichkeiten:

- Verb + Adverb

  *increase slightly, drop drastically, grow steadily*

  Das Adverb steht nach dem Verb.

- Adjektiv + Substantiv
  *sudden fall, dramatic increase, gradual decline*
- Adjektiv + Adverb
  *extremely good, considerably fast, surprisingly slow*
  Das Adverb steht vor dem Adjektiv.

### ☑ Rise und raise

Beachten Sie den Unterschied zwischen diesen Verben:

- *to rise* = (auf)steigen
  - Petrol prices **rose** again in May.
- *to raise sth* = etwas erhöhen
  - The oil industry **raised** prices last year.

### ☑ Zahlen

Wenn Sie in Ihrer Präsentation Zahlen nennen, beachten Sie folgende Regeln im Englischen:

1. Das Komma trennt Tausender-Einheiten und wird nicht ausgesprochen, z.B. 157,239.
2. Ein Punkt zeigt die Dezimalstelle, z.B. 1.7, und wird als *point* vorgelesen.
3. Die Wörter *million* und *billion* haben normalerweise kein Plural-s.
4. *Billion* (englisch) = Milliarde (deutsch)
5. Währungen können ein Plural-s haben, z.B. *10 dollars, 100 pounds.* Der Euro kann im Plural sowohl mit s (*20 euros*) als auch ohne s (*20 euro*) verwendet werden.

☞ **And by the way ...:** Große Zahlen kürzt man so ab: *million* = m (2m), *billion* = bn (1bn). Tausend stellt man oft als K dar: 4K = 4000. Das Zahlenkürzel wird normalerweise ohne Leerzeichen an die Zahl angefügt: $10m oder €1.5bn.

## 2.3 Vokabeln und Redewendungen auf einen Blick

### Wichtige Medien und Visualisierungsmittel

| | |
|---|---|
| Beamer | data projector |
| Bildschirm | screen |
| Dia, Präsentationsfolie | slide |
| Flipchart | flip chart |
| Flussdiagramm | flowchart |
| Folie | transparency |
| Karte, Plan | map |
| Kunststofftafel | whiteboard |
| Kurve | graph |
| Organigramm | organizational chart |
| Overheadprojektor | overhead projector (OHP) |
| Pinnwand | pin board |
| Säulendiagramm | bar chart |
| Strukturbild, Diagramm | diagram |
| Tabelle, Tafel | table |
| Technische Zeichnung | technical drawing |
| Tortendiagramm | pie chart |

### Visualisierungsmittel und Medien vorstellen

- As you can see here, …
- Let's now look at the next slide which shows …
- To illustrate this, let's have a closer look at …
- The chart on the following slide shows …
- I have a slide here that/which shows …
- The problem is illustrated in the next bar chart …
- According to this graph, our net profit has doubled.
- You can see the test results in this table.

## Grafiken erklären

- First, let me quickly explain the graph.
- You can see that different colours have been used to indicate …
- The new models are listed across the bottom.
- The biggest segment indicates …
- The key in the bottom left-hand corner shows you …
- The blue line gives us …
- In the upper right-hand corner you will see …

## Trends beschreiben

### 1 Nützliche Adjektive und Adverbien

| Deutsch | Adjektiv | Adverb |
|---|---|---|
| beträchtlich | considerable | considerably |
| dramatisch | dramatic | dramatically |
| drastisch | drastic | drastically |
| entscheidend | significant | significantly |
| heftig | sharp | sharply |
| leicht | slight | slightly |
| mäßig | moderate | moderately |
| plötzlich | sudden | suddenly |
| schrittweise | gradual | gradually |
| stetig | steady | steadily |

- Sales increased slightly in summer.
- Consumer spending fell/declined sharply.
- Interest rates have risen steadily.
- Food prices went up significantly.
- There was a sudden increase in prices.
- In August, we saw a moderate fall.
- This was followed by a gradual decline.
- There was a sharp slump in sales.

## 2 Nützliche Verben

| **Tendenz steigend** | | **Tendenz fallend** | |
|---|---|---|---|
| klettern | to climb | fallen | to drop, to fall |
| steigen | to rise | | |
| expandieren | to expand | abnehmen, zurückgehen | to decline |
| hochgehen | to go up | heruntergehen | to go down |
| wachsen | to grow | schrumpfen | to shrink |
| zunehmen | to increase | abnehmen | to decrease |
| in die Höhe schießen | to rocket | (ab)stürzen | to plunge, to slump |
| verbessern | to improve | sich verschlechtern | to deteriorate |
| sich erholen | to pick up, to recover | | |
| **Weitere Verben** | | | |
| stabil bleiben | to remain stable | schwanken | to fluctuate |
| Höchststand erreichen | to reach a high | Tiefpunkt erreichen | to hit a low |

## 2.4 Übungen

**Ü1 Setzen Sie die passenden Wörter und Ausdrücke ein.**

can see – next slide – page – on the board – a look – have a – illustration – go back – just flip

**Presentation 1**

1. Take ______________ at these figures.
2. I'll just write some figures _________________ and then we will go on to discuss the next point.

**Presentation 2**

3. OK. Let's now _________________ look at our new magnetic ski rack.
4. On the _____________________ you will see an __________________ of the Matterhorn X-15.

**Presentation 3**

5. As you ___________________ here, we've had a very successful year.
6. Let's ___________________ to the 2003 figures on the previous ___________________. Let me _______________ back to it.

### Ü2 Setzen Sie die Satzteile richtig zusammen.

| | |
|---|---|
| 1. On the next page | a from this picture, the design is absolutely new. |
| 2. My next slide shows | b users have complained about the service. |
| 3. As you can see | c how much the market has changed. |
| 4. I have a slide | d I'll show you our latest poster. |
| 5. To illustrate this | e you will see a photo of the new XTK model. |
| 6. Here we can see how many | f which shows the market development in 2005. |

### Ü3 Setzen Sie die passenden Wörter ein.

blue – left-hand – colours – line – explain – look at – indicate – attention

Let's now have a ____________ (1) the sales figures over the past five years. First, let me quickly ____________ (2) the graph. You can see that different ____________ (3) have been used to ____________ (4) each of our main sales areas. The key in the bottom ____________ (5) corner shows you which colour represents which area. The red ____________ (6), for example, gives us the sales figures for Belgium, the green line is for Germany and so on. OK, so I'd like to first draw your ____________ (7) to the sales figures for France – that's the ____________ (8) line here.

## Ü4 Setzen Sie die passenden Wörter ein.

account – amount – divided – see – shown – surprised – total

This pie chart shows our total health spending for the last year and how it is ______________ ❶ among the various health sector areas. Let's begin with the biggest area which is ______________ ❷ in green. We can ______________ ❸ that 31% of our total health spending went into hospital care last year. The second biggest area with a ______________ ❹ of 23% is 'other spending' – that's the red segment here. It includes dental services and home health care. I think you'll be ______________ ❺ to see that nearly the same ______________ ❻ – that's 22% – was spent on doctors and clinical services. This was mainly because of the increase in medical technology costs. Prescription drugs ______________ ❼ for 10% of our total costs.

## Ü5 Bilden Sie neue Sätze mit gerundeten Zahlen.

**Beispiel:** 1. Last year we sold 90,083 mobile phones.
~ *... we sold just over/about 90,000 mobile phones.*

2. 14.8% of the people asked said they were unhappy with the new design. ______________________________
______________________________
3. We will be spending €1.98m on it. ______________
______________________________
4. The ideal temperature is 18.1°C. ______________
______________________________
5. The new office is 389 m². ______________________
______________________________

## Ü6 Bilden Sie Sätze im Simple Past oder Present Perfect.

**Beispiel:** net profit / decrease / in the past two years
~ *Net profit has decreased in the past two years.*

1. telephone costs / rise / since January

   ________________________________________

2. sales / drop / at the beginning of the year

   ________________________________________

3. income tax / increase / over the past 30 years

   ________________________________________

4. gas prices / go up / last month

   ________________________________________

5. the number of customers / grow / since 2004

   ______________________________________

6. surprisingly / interest rates / fall / yesterday

   ______________________________________

## Ü7 Ergänzen Sie die richtige Verb-Adverb-Kombination in der richtigen Zeitform.

rise sharply – decrease steadily – ~~increase slightly~~ – fall dramatically – grow considerably – decline gradually

1. (↗) The line graph shows that car sales ***have increased slightly*** since May. (leicht)

2. (↓)You can see here that interest rates ______________________ at the beginning of 2004. (dramatisch)

3. (↘) Over the past six years, sales ____________________. (schrittweise)

4. (↑) The oil price ________________ after the fire in an oilfield. (heftig)

5. (↗) The number of online stores ________________________ this year. (beachtlich)

6. (↘) Our sales force ___________________________ since 2001. (stetig)

**Ü8 Setzen Sie die Satzteile richtig zusammen.**

| | |
|---|---|
| 1. Let's now have a look | a shows our revenues since 2004. ☐ |
| 2. The black line gives us | b at how the new division will be structured. ☐ |
| 3. Each line on the graph indicates | c you can see the specifications for the TP model. ☐ |
| 4. In the upper right-hand corner | d the sales figures for the VW Fox. ☐ |
| 5. The graph on the following slide | e across the top. ☐ |
| 6. The names of the new models are listed | f the production output of a different product. ☐ |

**Ü9 Setzen Sie die passenden Wörter ein.**

decline – fluctuated – picking up – reached – rose – slumped

1. As you can see here, passenger numbers ____________ between 2.1 and 2.3 million in the first four months.
2. They even ____________ moderately in May.
3. In June you'll notice a sharp ______________ in passenger numbers.
4. Passenger traffic ____________ to about 1.5 million.
5. As a result, ticket sales started _____________ in July.
6. By the end of September passenger numbers had ______________ just over 2 million.

**Ü10 Finden Sie ein Verb, das das Gegenteil bedeutet. Manchmal sind mehrere Lösungen möglich.**

1. to rise ______________________________
2. to hit a low ______________________________
3. to fluctuate ______________________________
4. to go up ______________________________
5. to improve ______________________________
6. to decrease ______________________________

# Fit for Presenting in English? Test Yourself!

## T1 Setzen Sie die richtigen Wörter ein.

bar – shows – see – this chart – look – segment – left – slide

1. The next ____________ shows the breakdown by age in our company.

2. You can __________ that the biggest ________ indicates the percentage of employees in the age group 30 to 50.

3. Now I'd like you to ___________ at ____________ which ___________ our turnover in 2006.

4. If you look at the ________ chart on the ____________, you will see an increase of 20 %.

## T2 Setzen Sie die richtigen Präpositionen ein.

around – at – between – by – from – in – of – to – until

The graph shows our online sales figures for the EU market __________ (1) 2004. In the first quarter, online sales averaged __________ (2) 50,000 and 52,000 euros. In April, sales increased __________ (3) 61,000 euros and remained steady __________ (4) the end of the second quarter. In the third quarter we notice a sharp rise __________ (5) 61,000 to 87,000 euros, an increase __________ (6) almost 50 %.
In October and November, sales fluctuated __________ (7) the 85,000 euro mark. This was followed by a slight decline in December, with online sales falling __________ (8) 10 %, reaching 73,000 euros __________ (9) the end of the year.

**T3 Welche dieser Sätze sind korrekt, welche nicht? Verbessern Sie die Fehler.**

1. We haven't raised prices since 1 January 2003.
2. Unemployment raised to a record high at the beginning of this year.
3. Why did they rise their rates last December?
4. Train fares in Germany have risen by 5 % in the past two years.
5. Interest rates will raise again this year.
6. The company rose the dividends in March.

**T4 Übersetzen Sie.**

1. Lassen Sie uns jetzt diese Tabelle näher betrachten.
2. Auf der nächsten Folie sehen Sie die Verkaufszahlen für das erste Quartal.
3. Dieses Tortendiagramm zeigt unseren Marktanteil in Prozent.
4. Ich würde gern Ihre Aufmerksamkeit auf folgende Fakten lenken.
5. Laut der Studie sind die Reisekosten seit 2000 stark gestiegen.
6. Unsere Produktivität erreichte im Dezember einen Tiefpunkt.

**T5 Wählen Sie die richtige Lösung.**

1. Productivity · has hit a low / has gone down / fell · in November.

2. Output · climbed up / has improved / recovered · since 2003.

3. After the takeover in May sales · grew up / have decreased / plunged.

4. This year our market share · raised / has grown / dropped down · by 10%.

5. Staff numbers · have doubled / rose up / have raised · this year.

6. In 2004 sales · have climbed / slumped / have risen.

# 3 Der Hauptteil einer Präsentation

## 3.1 Konkrete Präsentationssituationen

### Signposting: Sie führen das Publikum durch die Präsentation

Am Anfang des Hauptteils Ihrer Präsentation erklären Sie nochmals, was die Teilnehmer erwartet und in welcher Reihenfolge Sie vorgehen. Dann informieren Sie das Publikum an jeder Stelle des Vortrags, was als Nächstes geschieht.

**Sie stellen das Thema noch einmal kurz vor**
Zunächst geben Sie einen kurzen inhaltlichen Überblick.

- In this part of my presentation, I'd like to talk about ...
- So, let me first give you a brief overview.

**Überleiten zum nächsten Punkt**
Mit folgenden Sätzen können Sie zur nächsten Aussage überleiten:

- This leads directly to the next part of my talk.
- Let's now turn to ...
- This brings us to the next point.
- After looking at this point, let's now move on to ...

**Sie gelangen ans Ende eines Abschnitts**
Bereiten Sie das Publikum auf das Ende eines Gedankenganges oder Abschnitts vor, indem Sie z.B. sagen:

- This brings me to the end of my first point.
- So much for point two.
- That's all I wanted to say about ...

**Sie verweisen auf frühere Aussagen**
Häufig ist es hilfreich, Aussagen zu wiederholen oder noch einmal in einem anderen Zusammenhang auf sie zu verweisen. Um einen Satz einzuleiten, verwendet man häufig das Wort *as:*

- As I said earlier, ...
- As I've already explained, ...
- As I pointed out in the first part of my talk, ...

Andere Möglichkeiten:

- Let's go back to what we were discussing earlier.
- Let me come back to what I said in section one.

### Sie fassen wichtige Aussagen zusammen

Am Ende eines Abschnitts fassen Sie immer die wichtigsten Aussagen und Punkte zusammen:

- I'd like to sum up the main points.
- Let me summarize what I've said so far.
- Before I move on, I'd like to recap the main ideas.

### Sie verweisen auf andere Aspekte

Wenn Sie auf noch nicht genannte Punkte, Ideen oder Aspekte hinweisen möchten, gibt es eine Reihe von Ausdrücken, die im Deutschen etwa mit *hinsichtlich* oder *bezüglich* übersetzt werden. Achten Sie in diesem Zusammenhang unbedingt auf die richtigen Präpositionen:

- in connection with (im Zusammenhang mit)
- with respect to (hinsichtlich)
- with regard to (in Bezug auf)
- according to (laut, gemäß)
- concerning/regarding (betreffend)
- with reference to (in Bezug auf)

- I'd like to mention some critical points in connection with / concerning payment.
- There are a few problems regarding the quality.
- With respect/regard to prices, we need more details.
- According to the survey, our customers are unhappy with this product.

### Sie fügen neue Ideen oder Argumente hinzu

Mit folgenden Ausdrücken führen Sie neue Punkte ein:

- in addition to (zusätzlich, darüber hinaus)
- additionally (zusätzlich)
- moreover (darüber hinaus)
- furthermore (des Weiteren)
- as well as that (genauso)
- apart from (abgesehen von)
- plus (zusätzlich, plus)

- In addition to this, I'd like to say that our IT business is going very well.
- Moreover/Furthermore, there are other interesting facts we should take a look at.
- As well as that, we can offer excellent conditions.
- Apart from being too expensive, this model is also too big.
- To increase sales we need a new strategy plus more people.

**Sie sprechen Probleme an**

Um schwierige Situationen zu erklären, werden gerne Verben wie diese verwendet:

- to identify (identifizieren)
- to deal with (umgehen mit, sich kümmern um)
- to clarify (klären)
- to cope with (fertig werden mit)
- to tackle (anpacken)
- to solve (lösen)
- to take care of (sich kümmern um)

- I think we first need to identify the problem.
- Of course we'll have to clarify a few points before we start.
- We will have to deal with the problem of increasing prices.
- How shall we cope with unfair business practices?
- The question is: why don't we tackle the distribution problems?
- If we don't solve this problem now, we'll get into serious trouble soon.
- We will have to take care of this problem now.

☞ **And by the way ...:** *Einerseits ... andererseits* heißt *on the one hand ... on the other hand* (nicht ~~side~~).

**Sie betonen wichtige Gesichtspunkte**
Wenn Sie etwas besonders hervorheben möchten, gibt es vier verschiedene Möglichkeiten:

- Mit einem Verb
  Geeignet sind z.B. *to stress, to emphasize* oder *to highlight,* die alle mit *betonen* oder *hervorheben* übersetzt werden:
  - I'd like to stress the following point.
  - I'd like to emphasize that our market position is excellent.

  Auch möglich sind *to draw* bzw. *to call s.o.'s attention to:*
  - I'd like to draw your attention to the latest figures.

- Mit *what* zu Beginn des Satzes
  - What is really important is how much we are prepared to invest.
  - What we should do is talk about intercultural problems.

- Mit einer rhetorischen Frage
  - So, just how good are the results?
  - So, where do we go from here?
  - Why do I say that? Because …

- Mit einer Adverb-Adjektiv-Kombination
  - It would be completely wrong to change our strategy at this point.
  - We compared the two offers and found the first one totally unacceptable.
  - I think this fact is extremely important.

**Sie erläutern Absicht und Zweck**
Wenn Sie erklären möchten, was Sie mit einer bestimmten Handlungsweise bezwecken oder bezweckt haben, verwenden Sie Ausdrücke wie *purpose* (Zweck, Absicht), *aim, goal* oder *objective* (Ziel):

- The purpose of this step is to ...
- Our aim was to ...
- We used this method to ...

**Sie erklären Ursache oder Grund**

Beachten Sie dabei die Verwendung der Präpositionen:

- cause of (Ursache von)
- caused by (verursacht von)
- because of (wegen)
- reason(s) for (Grund/Gründe für)
- therefore (deshalb)

Hier einige Beispiele:

- Let's have a look at the cause of this problem.
- This was caused by several factors.
- This was because of the delivery problems.
- What's the reason for this sudden increase?

**Sie beschreiben Auswirkung oder Ergebnis**

Wählen Sie einen dieser Ausdrücke:

- as a result (als Ergebnis)
- as a consequence (als Folge)
- consequently (folglich)
- to result in (resultieren in)
- to lead to (führen zu)
- to prompt (auslösen, veranlassen)
- thus (somit, folglich)

Einige Beispiele:

- As a result, profit went up by 20%.
- The takeover resulted in an increase in orders.
- This has led to better quality.
- The new law prompted us to act quickly.

**Sie beschreiben Gegensätze**

Wenn Sie Gegensätze oder Einschränkungen ausdrücken möchten, benutzen Sie folgende Wörter:

- on the one hand (einerseits), on the other hand (andererseits)
- on the contrary (im Gegenteil)
- whereas (wogegen)
- while (während)
- despite (trotz)
- although (obwohl)
- however (jedoch, allerdings)

Einige Beispiele:

- On the one hand, this was very positive. On the other hand, we lost a few good customers.
- Sales in our area were extremely good, whereas sales in France declined sharply.
- Our German market figures are bad while the global market is doing very well.
- Despite the growing demand in China, we weren't able to improve our Asian export business.
- There is, however, another important point.

## 3.2 Präsentationsstrategien und interkulturelle Aspekte

**Signposting im Hauptteil Ihrer Präsentation**

Auch wenn es Ihnen übertrieben erscheint: Beachten Sie die Signposting-Regeln, die im angloamerikanischen Sprachraum üblich sind. Lassen Sie die Teilnehmer an jeder Stelle Ihres Vortrages deutlich wissen, wo genau sie sich befinden und was sie als Nächstes erwartet. Das bedeutet für den Mittelteil Ihrer Präsentation im Einzelnen:

1. Beginnen Sie mit einer kurzen Erläuterung des Themas und Zwecks Ihrer Präsentation.
2. Weisen Sie auf den Beginn eines neuen Punktes hin.
3. Signalisieren Sie das Ende jedes Abschnitts oder Unterpunktes.
4. Fassen Sie jeweils am Ende eines Abschnitts die wichtigsten Ergebnisse zusammen.

**Kommunikationsstil in den USA und Deutschland**

Kommunikation ist in der internationalen Geschäftswelt ein wichtiger Schlüssel zum Erfolg. Zahlreiche Studien belegen, dass viele Geschäftsabschlüsse mit ausländischen Firmen an schlechter Kommunikation scheitern – in einer entsprechenden Studie vor ein paar Jahren waren es sogar sieben von zehn!

Da Kommunikation aber nicht nur mit Sprache zu tun hat, sondern auch mit dem jeweiligen kulturellen oder sozialen Hintergrund, kommt es hier leicht zu falschen Einschätzungen.

> Denken Sie immer daran, dass jeder von uns kulturell konditioniert ist.

D.h., wir halten bestimmte Verhaltens- und Vorgehensweisen für normal, richtig oder angebracht und versuchen mit diesem Maßstab, fremde Verhaltensweisen zu bewerten. Das kann ins Auge gehen!

### ☑ Interkulturelle Probleme bei Präsentationen am Beispiel USA – Deutschland

Am Beispiel des Zusammenschlusses von Daimler-Benz und Chrysler lässt sich anschaulich demonstrieren, wie trotz bester Absichten selbst bei Weltkonzernen erhebliche Probleme in der Kommunikation auftreten können:
Für das erste Treffen nach der Fusion 1998 wurde vereinbart, dass jede Seite sich in einer Präsentation vorstellen sollte.
Die Deutschen präsentierten zwei Stunden lang, zeigten viele Folien, gaben einen ausführlichen Überblick über Firmengeschichte, Produktpalette und zukünftige Vorhaben.
Der Vortrag der Amerikaner dauerte 25 Minuten, konzentrierte sich ausschließlich auf die Vorstellung der Firmenprodukte und war mit vielen Spezialeffekten aufbereitet. Die Sprache war einfach, die Sätze einprägsam.
Während der Deutsche mit steifer Körperhaltung und monotoner Stimme sprach, war der Amerikaner lebhaft und seine Stimme voller Begeisterung.
Welchen Eindruck der deutsche Präsentationsstil auf die amerikanische Seite machte, äußerte der damalige Vorstandsvorsitzende Robert Eaton in einem Interview. Darin beklagte er sich, dass die Deutschen immer tonnenweise Folien und Farbgrafiken einsetzten. Seinen Eindruck schilderte er mit den Worten *absolute information overkill.*

**Kulturelle Unterschiede, die Sie kennen sollten**

Wenn Sie in einem angloamerikanischen Umfeld präsentieren, sollten Sie auf Folgendes achten:

### ☑ Sachlichkeit und Publikumswirkung

Während bei deutschen Präsentationen meist Inhalt, Sachlichkeit und Wahrheitsfindung im Mittelpunkt stehen, bringen Amerikaner viel stärker auch persönliche Aspekte ein. Meist sind sie auch mehr an einer Außenwirkung interessiert und suchen nach Anerkennung durch das Publikum.

### ☑ Lob und Kritik

Deutsche sind oft sehr direkt – vor allem, wenn es um negative Einschätzungen oder Kritik geht. Amerikaner äußern dagegen positive Dinge und Lob oft und direkt, Kritik wird aber meist in vorsichtige Formulierungen verpackt.

> Mit offener Kritik an Personen, Firmen, Institutionen und amerikanischen Werten sollte man sich zurückhalten.

### ☑ Humor

Von einer positiven und optimistischen Grundhaltung ausgehend, ist für Amerikaner Humor ein wichtiger Bestandteil eines Vortrages. Eine Präsentation beginnt deshalb oft mit einem Witz oder einer lustigen Geschichte. Von deutscher Seite wird dies oft als oberflächlich oder als Ablenkung empfunden.

### ☑ Körpersprache

In der Regel nutzen Amerikaner in viel stärkerem Maße die Möglichkeit, durch Körpersprache ihre Präsentation zu unterstützen und ihre Botschaft dem Publikum zu vermitteln. Hollywoodreife Gestikulation wird aber vom deutschen Publikum meist nicht geschätzt.

### ☑ Handlungsorientierung

Amerikaner sind in der Regel äußerst handlungsorientiert und pragmatisch. In einem Vortrag zeigt sich das darin, dass man schnell zum wesentlichen Punkt kommt. Wichtige Botschaften werden zuerst genannt und auch gern wiederholt. Der vielversprechendste Lösungsansatz wird in die Praxis umgesetzt, bevor man sich mit Details und etwaigen Bedenken auseinandergesetzt hat.

> ☞ **And by the way ...:** Die Lösung eines Problems heißt *solution **to** a problem* (nicht ~~*of a problem*~~).

## 3.3 Vokabeln und Redewendungen auf einen Blick

**Das Thema noch einmal kurz vorstellen**

- In this part of my presentation, I'd like to talk about …
- So, let me first give you a brief overview.

**Zum nächsten Punkt überleiten**

- This leads directly to my next point.
- This brings us to the next question.
- Let's now move on / turn to …
- After examining this point, let's turn to …
- Let's now take a look at …

**Das Ende eines Abschnitts ankündigen**

- This brings me to the end of my first point.
- So much for point two.
- So, that's the background on …
- That's all I wanted to say about …

**Auf frühere Aussagen verweisen**

- As I said/mentioned earlier, …
- Let me come back to what I said before …
- Let's go back to what we were discussing earlier.
- As I've already explained, …
- As I pointed out in the first section, …

**Wichtige Aussagen zusammenfassen**

- Before I move on, I'd like to recap the main points.
- Let me briefly summarize the main issues.
- I'd like to summarize what I've said so far …

### Auf weitere Aspekte verweisen

- I have a question in connection with / concerning payment.
- There are a few problems regarding the quality.
- With respect/regard to planning, we need more background information.
- According to the survey, our customer service needs reviewing.

### Neue Ideen und Argumente hinzufügen

- In addition to this, I'd like to say that our IT business is going very well.
- Moreover/Furthermore, there are other interesting facts we should take a look at.
- Apart from being too expensive, this model is too big.

### Probleme ansprechen

- I think we first need to identify the problem.
- Of course we'll have to clarify a few points before we start.
- We'll have to deal with the problem of increasing prices.
- How will we cope with unfair business practices?
- The question is: why don't we tackle the distribution problems?
- If we don't solve this problem now, we'll get/run into serious trouble soon.
- We'll have to take care of this problem now.
- We're currently having difficulties with …

### Wichtige Aspekte betonen

- I'd like to stress/highlight/emphasize the following point(s).
- I'd like to start by drawing your attention to …
- Let me point out that …
- I think you'll be surprised to see that …
- I'd like you to focus your attention on …
- What's really important here is …
- What I'd like to point out here is …
- Let's look more closely at …

### Schlussfolgerungen ziehen

- What conclusion can we draw from this?
- So, what does this mean?
- So, just how good are the results?
- So, how are we going to deal with this increase?

### Absicht und Zweck erläutern

- We introduced this method to increase flexibility.
- The purpose of this step is to expand to foreign markets.
- Our aim was to improve our services.

### Ursache oder Grund erklären

- What's the reason for this drastic decrease?
- The unexpected drop was caused by the oil crisis.
- This was because of bad economic conditions.

**Folgen beschreiben**

- As a consequence / Consequently, sales went up significantly.
- As a result we reached more customers.
- The venture resulted in a sharp fall in share prices.
- Our new strategy has led to an increase of 10%.

**Gegensätze beschreiben**

- Last year's figures were very good, whereas sales this year have gone down by 12%.
- We mainly export goods to Asia, while they sell to the US.
- Despite the good conditions they offered, we couldn't agree to the deal.
- The US is the global market leader. We are, however, the market leader in Europe.

## 3.4 Übungen

**Ü1 Bilden Sie vollständige Sätze. Benutzen Sie für jeden Satz jede Spalte.**

| | | |
|---|---|---|
| 1. As I said earlier, | come back to | my next question. |
| 2. This brings | the issue | which is price. |
| 3. This leads to | let me go | this question later. |
| 4. Let's now turn to | what we were discussing | on our new sales strategies. |
| 5. As I mentioned before, | the next point, | a brief overview of our activities. |
| 6. I'd like to | I'd like to give you | earlier. |
| 7. Let's go back to | us directly to | through the main issues once more. |
| 8. Before I move on to my next point, | I'll be focussing | of customer service. |

**Ü2 Setzen Sie den passenden Ausdruck ein.**

according to – apart from – concerns – moreover – regarding – with regard

1. I'll give you an overview of some figures ________________ to car exports.

2. ________________, I'd like to tell you something about the new software.

3. Let's now turn to the next question which ________________ customer service.

4. ________________ a few spelling mistakes, the new brochure is very good.

5. Let me give you some details ________________ our Chinese factory.

6. ________________ the handbook, the scanner is user-friendly.

**Ü3 Fügen Sie die Satzteile richtig zusammen.**

| | |
|---|---|
| 1. There are several reasons | a our sales went up! |
| 2. We chose this method because | b new overtime policy. |
| 3. The result | c by the collapse of one of our partner firms. |
| 4. Our new policy has led | d of this move was a drastic increase in our costs. |
| 5. The slump was caused | e to a significant rise in sales. |
| 6. Downsizing resulted | f we needed reliable figures. |
| 7. We increased our prices and | g for the decrease in productivity. |
| 8. Our output has doubled thanks to | h in a drastic fall in staff numbers. |

**Ü4 Bilden Sie Sätze mit *as*. Verwenden Sie die Informationen in Klammern und ergänzen Sie fehlende Wörter wo nötig.**

**Beispiel:**

1. we / no budget for new software / this year (I mentioned this before)
   ~ *As I mentioned before, we have no budget for new software this year.*
2. Tony Dale / new marketing manager / print media (you all know this already)
   ______________________________________________
3. can't operate from local airport / because no permission (I said this at the beginning of my talk)
   ______________________________________________
4. choose between two options (I explained this ten minutes ago)
   ______________________________________________
5. sales have increased / 10% since beginning of year (you can see this on the slide)
   ______________________________________________

**Ü5 Setzen Sie den passenden Ausdruck ein.**

extremely dangerous – absolutely safe – incredibly cheap – highly interesting – absolutely necessary – surprisingly good – completely useless

1. What we should remember is that this chemical process is ______________________.
2. It's ______________________ to improve the quality of our products if we want to win new customers.

3. This is a ______________________ point.

4. You will be pleased to hear that our turnover last month was ______________________.

5. Unfortunately, we found that some of the test results are ______________________.

6. I'm pleased to say that the crash test shows that this system is ______________________.

7. Right now this item only costs $1.50 – I think that's ______________________.

**Ü6 Setzen Sie den passenden Ausdruck ein.**

let's talk about – draw your attention – have a look – it's quite remarkable – on the other hand – the figures also show that – you will see – can we explain

I'd now like to ______________ (1) to the regions where poverty has been reduced. If you look at the bar chart on the left, ______________ (2) that the proportion of global population living on less than $1 a day has dropped. ______________ (3) in South Asia the proportion of extremely poor people has been reduced from 41 to 31%. ______________ (4) how much progress has been made by China. ______________ (5), poverty has increased in many parts of Africa, Latin America and Eastern Europe. How ______________ (6) this uneven development? To answer this question, we'll ______________ (7) at the latest study from the World Bank. First, ______________ (8) the figures that indicate global progress.

### Ü7 Setzen Sie das passende Verb in der richtigen Form ein.

accept – cope – deal – have – identify – prevent – run – not solve

As you probably know, we ________ currently ________ (1) difficulties with our new men's cosmetic line. I'd like to quickly ________ (2) the problems and then make some suggestions on how we can ________ (3) with the consequences. We've been trying to ________ (4) with these problems – the delays, the poor quality – all along, but so far we've not been able to find ways to ________ (5) them from happening again. It's clear we can no longer continue to ________ (6) these conditions. If we ________ (7) our supply problems within the next two weeks, we ________ (8) into serious trouble with respect to our Christmas business.

### Ü8 Fügen Sie die Satzteile richtig zusammen.

1. What I'd like to do
2. I'd like to highlight the
3. So, what are the reasons
4. I'd like to point out how
5. It's interesting to note that
6. I should repeat that our
7. What we can't do is
8. So, just how good

a important advertising is for us.
b for our success?
c this model is selling quite well in the US.
d turnover last year was excellent.
e is discuss the latest sales figures.
f is the quality of these programs?
g main problem areas.
h increase our budget.

## Fit for Presenting in English?
## Test Yourself!

**T1 Setzen Sie den passenden Ausdruck ein.**

back – covered – discussing – inform – leads –
main points – sum up – wanted

1. Let me now summarize the ________________.

2. We will be ________________ our sales targets today.

3. In my talk I'll ________________ you about new marketing techniques.

4. Before I move on, let me just ________________ what I've said so far.

5. I think we have ________________ everything for today.

6. OK, that's all I ________________ to say about time management.

7. This ________________ directly to my second point.

8. Let's go ________________ to what I said at the beginning of my presentation.

## T2 Wählen Sie das richtige Verb aus.

1. How are we going to solve/deal/tackle with delivery problems?
2. I don't think we can cope / tackle / take care with fewer people.
3. We think it's important to identify/deal/cope the problems now.
4. Who will take care / deal / tackle of our business clients?
5. We have been trying to cope / solve / take care the software problem.
6. Before we go on, let's identify/clarify/solve this question.

## T3 Übersetzen Sie.

1. Lassen Sie uns jetzt zum nächsten Punkt übergehen.
2. Trotz der Softwareprobleme konnten wir ein überraschend gutes Ergebnis erzielen.
3. Der Grund für den Rückgang ist die schlechte Wirtschaftslage.
4. Ich möchte gern betonen, wie wichtig diese Änderung ist.
5. Wie ich bereits erwähnte, gebe ich Ihnen zunächst einen kurzen Überblick.
6. Andererseits müssen wir uns um die Konsequenzen kümmern.

**T4 Wählen Sie den richtigen Ausdruck aus.**

1. Online banking is mainly used by our younger customers. Many of our older customers consequently/however/therefore find it difficult to handle modern computer technology.

2. However/Whereas/Although the euro is quite strong, we managed to increase our exports to the US.

3. Whereas/Therefore/Despite we made a profit of $240,000 last year, this year's profit is only $110,000.

4. On the other hand / Despite / Although the growing demand, we didn't sell more cars than the year before.

5. We have to pay more for oil and gas. Consequently/However/Despite our products have become more expensive.

6. Poster campaigns are extremely important. Thus / On the other hand / As a result we also need advertisements in daily newspapers.

# 4 Der Schlussteil

## 4.1 Konkrete Präsentationssituationen

**Sie signalisieren das Ende des Vortrags**
Wie in den anderen Teilen Ihrer Präsentation kündigen Sie auch hier die nächsten Schritte an. Um auf das Ende Ihres Vortrags vorzubereiten, sagen Sie:

- Well, this brings me to the end of my presentation.
- I'm now nearing the end of my talk.
- Well, I'm now approaching the end of my presentation.
- OK, I think that's everything I wanted to say ...
- As a final point, I'd like to ...

**Sie fassen die wichtigsten Ergebnisse zusammen**

Geben Sie am Schluss Ihres Vortrags einen Überblick über die wichtigsten Punkte und fassen Sie kurz Resultate oder Erkenntnisse zusammen.

Mit den folgenden beiden Sätzen können Sie den vorherigen Punkt mit dieser Ankündigung verbinden:

- Before I stop, let me go through my main points again.
- Before I end my presentation today, I'd like to briefly recap the main points.

Das deutsche Verb *zusammenfassen* können Sie folgendermaßen übersetzen:

- to summarize
- to sum up
- to recap

Auch diese Verben können Sie einsetzen:

- to go/run through (durchgehen)
- to go/come back to (zurückgehen zu, zurückkommen auf)

Wenn Sie wichtige Punkte, Ergebnisse etc. erwähnen wollen, sind folgende Ausdrücke nützlich:

- main/key points
- key issues/questions (Punkte, Fragen)
- main results/findings (Ergebnisse)
- main options (Möglichkeiten)

Hier einige Beispielsätze:

- To sum up then, we ...
- Just to summarize the main points of my talk ...
- I'll just run through the three different options ...
- Let me just go through the key issues again.
- Finally, let me come back to the key points of my talk.

### Sie machen einen Vorschlag oder geben eine Empfehlung

Schlagen Sie eine Vorgehensweise oder Möglichkeit vor.

- We'd suggest ...
- What I'd like to suggest is ...
- We'd therefore recommend that we ...
- In my opinion, we should ...
- I'm convinced that we need ...
- After weighing the pros and cons, we think a merger would be the best option.

Beachten Sie, dass es beim Verb *suggest* nur folgende Einsatzmöglichkeiten gibt:

◆ *to suggest* + *that* + Infinitiv (ohne *to*)

  - We suggest that we continue ...
  - I suggest that you go on ...

  Mit dieser Form können Sie mehrere Subjekte im Satz verwenden. (**Ich** schlage vor, dass **Sie** ...)

◆ *to suggest* + Verb in der *-ing*-Form (Gerundium)

  - We suggest having another meeting in June.

  Hier gibt es nur ein Subjekt. (**Wir** schlagen vor etwas zu tun, bzw. dass **wir** etwas tun.)

### Sie bieten dem Publikum an, Fragen zu stellen

Haben Sie am Ende des Vortrags eine Fragezeit vorgesehen, signalisieren Sie nun, dass Fragen gestellt werden dürfen.

- Now I'll be happy to answer any questions you may have. Yes?
- Are there any questions?
- We just have time for a few questions.

☞ **And by the way ...:** Beachten Sie, dass es im Englischen *to recommend something **to** someone* heißt.

## Alternativen für den Schlussteil

### ☑ Sie stellen eine (provokative) Frage

- After all, isn't that why we're here?
- Let me just finish with a question: If we don't do it, won't somebody else?
- So, do we really want to miss this opportunity to get ahead of our competitors?

### ☑ Sie zitieren eine bekannte Person

Benutzen Sie ein Zitat, um Ihre Aussage zu unterstützen.

- As ... once said, ...
- To quote a well-known businessman, ...
- To put it in the words of ... , ...

### ☑ Sie verweisen auf den Anfang Ihres Vortrages

Verbinden Sie ein Element vom Anfang Ihrer Präsentation mit dem Schlussteil, indem Sie nun darauf Bezug nehmen.

- Remember what I said at the beginning of my talk today?
- Well, perhaps you remember what I said at the beginning of my talk ...
- Let me just go back to the story I told you earlier.
- Remember, ...

### ☑ Sie fordern zum Handeln auf

Im Englischen nennt man es *call to action* (oder *call for action*), wenn man den Teilnehmern am Schluss noch einmal direkt sagt, was von ihnen erwartet wird.

- OK, and now let's get down to work!
- So that's the plan. Now let's go and put it into practice!
- So now it's your turn.
- Now let's make a real effort to achieve this goal!

## 4.2 Präsentationsstrategien und interkulturelle Aspekte

Wie in den anderen Teilen Ihres Vortrags ist es auch hier wichtig, einen klaren Übergang herzustellen. Verwenden Sie also wieder einen Signposting-Satz, damit die Teilnehmer wissen, dass nun der letzte Teil des Vortrags beginnt.

**Hinterlassen Sie einen guten Eindruck!**
Viele Fachleute sagen, dass der Schluss einer Präsentation ebenso wichtig ist wie der Anfang. Andere gehen noch weiter und halten den Schluss für noch wichtiger. Das liegt daran, dass man sich normalerweise das am besten merkt, was man zuletzt gehört hat.

**Hinterlassen Sie einen bleibenden Eindruck!**
Der Schlussteil des Vortrags ist eine letzte Chance, um sicherzustellen, dass das Publikum die wichtigsten Ideen und Aussagen Ihrer Präsentation tatsächlich aufgenommen hat. Wiederholen Sie also noch einmal in prägnanter Form die Kernaussagen, damit Ihr Publikum sie sich merken kann.

**Den Schlussteil gestalten**
Da der Schlussteil so wichtig ist, achten Sie ganz besonders auf seine Gestaltung. Wie Sie vorgehen, ist Ihre Entscheidung. Richten Sie sich dabei nach Thema und Zielsetzung Ihres Vortrags und der Zusammensetzung Ihres Publikums.

☑ **Die wichtigsten Punkte zusammenfassen**
Dies ist die wohl gängigste und gleichzeitig am wenigsten einfallsreiche Methode, die aber in vielen Situationen völlig ausreichend ist.

☑ **Eine bekannte Person zitieren**
Vor allem bei Amerikanern ist dies eine sehr beliebte Methode. Dabei werden häufig Personen zitiert, die in Politik, Wirtschaft oder Sport besondere Leistungen erbracht haben. Mit einem Zitat können Sie Ihre Aussage unterstützen und sie gleichzeitig interessanter erscheinen lassen.

> Achten Sie aber darauf, dass das Zitat wirklich zu hundert Prozent zu Ihrer Aussage passt!

Im Internet finden Sie eine Menge Zitate bekannter Persönlichkeiten – suchen Sie zum Beispiel unter dem Stichwort *quotations*, *famous quotes* oder *proverbs*.

> ☞ **And by the way …:** *At the end* und *in the end* haben unterschiedliche Bedeutungen! *At the end of a presentation/report/meeting/…* bedeutet *am Ende von etwas*. *In the end* bedeutet *schließlich, zum Schluss*.

☑ **Eine überraschende Aussage oder eine provokative Frage**
Stellen Sie am Ende Ihrer Präsentation eine Frage oder machen Sie eine Aussage, die das Publikum überrascht oder provoziert und Ihre Hauptaussage unterstützt. Auch dies ist eine Methode, die im amerikanischen Sprachraum häufiger eingesetzt wird als bei uns.

☑ **Die Sandwich-Technik**
Stellen Sie sich Ihren Vortrag wie ein Sandwich vor: Zwischen zwei Scheiben Brot (Einleitung und Schluss) befindet sich ein Stück Käse oder Wurst (Inhalt = Hauptteil).
Mit Sandwich-Technik ist gemeint, dass es eine Verbindung zwischen den einzelnen Teilen einer Präsentation gibt, vor allem zwischen Anfang und Schluss.
Wenn Sie also am Anfang einen Witz oder eine Geschichte begonnen haben, dann greifen Sie im Schlussteil den Faden wieder auf und spannen so einen Bogen über die gesamte Präsentation.

☑ **Dank an die Teilnehmer**
In den meisten Präsentationen bedankt sich der Vortragende am Ende für die Aufmerksamkeit der Teilnehmer. Es gibt Präsentationsexperten, die dies völlig ablehnen mit der Begründung, dass sich nach einer guten Präsentation das Publikum bei Ihnen bedanken sollte – nicht umgekehrt!

### Die Stimme bewusst einsetzen

Wenn Sie eine Präsentation als besonders wenig ansprechend und ermüdend empfanden, dann lag das mit Sicherheit auch an der Art und Weise, wie der Inhalt vorgetragen wurde.

> Wie Sie etwas sagen, ist genauso wichtig wie das, was Sie sagen!

Das interessanteste Thema wirkt langweilig, wenn es mit monotoner Stimme und ohne besondere Akzente vorgetragen wird. Nutzen Sie deshalb Ihre Stimme, um bestimmte Wörter hervorzuheben. Das belebt Ihren Vortrag und macht es für die Teilnehmer leichter, Ihnen zu folgen.

### ☑ Besondere Betonung

Durch das Hervorheben einzelner Wörter oder Silben können Sie bestimmte Effekte erzielen und die Bedeutung des Satzes verändern.
Vergleichen Sie die folgenden Aussagen, in denen der fett gedruckte Teil besonders betont wird:

- We all know that this is an **extremely** difficult market. (mehr als nur schwierig)
- We **all** know that this is an extremely difficult market. (wir sind uns alle einig)
- **We** all know that this is an extremely difficult market. (aber andere wissen es nicht)

Achten Sie darauf, dass Sie nicht Ihr deutsches Betonungsmuster übertragen, sondern tatsächlich die Wörter betonen, die Sie für besonders wichtig halten oder die in einem Satz eine besondere Bedeutung haben sollen.

### ☑ Pausen einfügen

Pausen können dabei helfen, das Tempo des Vortrags zu reduzieren und ihn für das Publikum verständlicher zu machen.
Bilden Sie also sinnvolle Einheiten von Wortgruppen, zwischen denen Sie eine kurze Pause einfügen. Die folgenden Sätze zeigen, wie das aussehen könnte:

- In my opinion | we should go | into other markets.
- On the other hand, | the figures prove | that we are on the right track.

## 4.3 Vokabeln und Redewendungen auf einen Blick

**Das Ende der Präsentation ankündigen**

- I'm now approaching/nearing the end of my presentation.
- Well, this brings me to the end of my presentation.
- That covers just about everything I wanted to say about …
- OK, I think that's everything I wanted to say about …
- As a final point, I'd like to …
- Finally, I'd like to highlight one key issue.

**Wesentliches zusammenfassen**

- Before I stop, let me go over the key issues again.
- Just to summarize the main points of my talk …
- I'd like to run through my main points again …
- To conclude / In conclusion, I'd like to …
- To sum up (then), we …

**Einen besonders wichtigen Punkt hervorheben**

- Let's go back to our key issue.
- Finally, let me highlight the key question once again.
- Let me emphasize the importance of … once again.

**Vorschläge machen und Empfehlungen geben**

- We'd suggest …
- We therefore (strongly) recommend that …
- My suggestion is …
- In my opinion, we should …
- Based on the figures we have, I'm quite certain that …

**Fragen zulassen**

- Are there any questions?
- We just have time for a few questions.
- And now I'll be happy to answer any questions you may have.

**Eine bekannte Person zitieren**

- As … once said, …
- To quote a well-known businessman, …
- To put it in the words of …

**Eine Verbindung zur Einleitung herstellen**

- Remember what I said at the beginning of my talk today?
- Let me just go back to the story I told you earlier. Remember, …
- Well, perhaps you remember what I said at the beginning of my talk …

**Die Teilnehmer zum Handeln auffordern**

- So that's the plan. Now let's go and put it into practice!
- So now it's your turn.
- OK, and now let's get down to work!
- Now let's make a real effort to achieve this goal!

## 4.4 Übungen

**Ü1 Setzen Sie die passenden Ausdrücke ein.**

come back – figures we have – final point – briefly summarize – my opinion – now approaching – suggest that – to highlight

1. If I may ______________________ the pros and cons.
2. Based on the ______________________, it is clear that we must act quickly.
3. Well, I'm ______________________ the end of my talk.
4. OK, I'd now like ______________________ the key figures.
5. Let me make one ______________________.
6. In ______________________, we need a new sales strategy.
7. Let me ______________________ to the key issue.
8. I ______________________ we work together with our French partners.

**Ü2 Unterstreichen Sie das Wort, das gemäß den Angaben in der Klammer betont werden soll.**

1. Clearly, we need to look at this again. (es ist offensichtlich!)
2. We will never get such a perfect opportunity again. (das ist unsere einzige Chance)

3. I'd like us to work out a strategy. (ein Plan ist wichtig)

4. There hasn't been a dramatic increase in production costs. (aber es hat einen Anstieg gegeben)

5. There hasn't been a dramatic increase in production costs. (aber andere Kosten sind gestiegen)

6. I think we've made a good start. (andere denken das vielleicht nicht)

**Ü3 Setzen Sie die richtige Präposition ein.**

about – by – for – in – on – out – through – to

1. Based ____________ what we know, we can optimize our procedures.

2. ____________ my opinion, we should go ahead with the project.

3. OK, this brings me ____________ the end of my talk.

4. What does this mean ____________ our business?

5. Let me just go ____________ the key issues again.

6. We found ____________ that our sales force needs more support.

7. Well, that's all I wanted to say ____________ strategic planning.

8. We saw that the delays were caused ____________ technical problems.

## Ü4 Setzen Sie die passenden Ausdrücke ein.

briefly recap – convinced that – key question – story – want to miss – remember

1. Let me go back to the ______________ I told you at the start of my talk. ______________, the sales meeting in Vienna with the disappointed Japanese businessmen?
2. So, to conclude, I'm ______________ ICM would be an excellent method to make better use of the knowledge we have.
   So, do we really ________________ this opportunity to get ahead of our competitors?
3. Finally, let me highlight the ______________ once again: do we need a digital telephone system or can we upgrade the existing one?
4. Before I end my presentation today, I'd like to ______________ the main reasons for doing business with us.

## Ü5 Bilden Sie vollständige Sätze.

1. Well, / the end of / today / brings me / to / my talk / that
   ________________________________________________
2. Before I / key issues / go over / the / stop, / let me / again
   ________________________________________________
3. As a / means / let me say / for us / what this / final point,
   ________________________________________________

4. Finally, / like to / issue / highlight / I'd / one / key

______________________________________________

5. To sum up / looked at / product range / then, / the new / first / we

______________________________________________

6. That / logistics / just about / to say / about / I wanted / everything / covers

______________________________________________

**Ü6 Fügen Sie die Satzteile richtig zusammen.**

| | | | |
|---|---|---|---|
| 1. | To put it in the words of Albert Einstein: | a | "Look for your choices, pick the best one, then go with it." ☐ |
| 2. | I would like to finish my talk | b | with an important question. ☐ |
| 3. | Let me go back to | c | about the new branch in Tokyo? ☐ |
| 4. | So, now it's | d | get down to work! ☐ |
| 5. | Remember that story I told you | e | what I said at the start of this talk. ☐ |
| 6. | As the famous basketball coach Pat Riley said: | f | "The important thing is not to stop questioning." ☐ |
| 7. | OK, and now let's | g | up to you. ☐ |

## Fit for Presenting in English?
## Test Yourself!

**T1 Ordnen Sie die Sätze den vier Themenbereichen zu.**

a Ende des Vortrags
b Zusammenfassung
c Vorschläge/Empfehlungen
d Fragen

1. I'll just run through the three different options once more. ☐
2. We'd suggest that you invest in new hardware. ☐
3. Now I'll be happy to answer any questions you may have. ☐
4. We'd therefore recommend that we use temporary staff. ☐
5. Before I stop, let me go through my main points again. ☐
6. Well, this brings me to the end of my presentation. ☐
7. We just have time for a few questions. ☐
8. In my opinion, we should reorganize the sales division. ☐

## T2 Setzen Sie die richtige Präposition ein.

for – from – of – with – on (2x) – in – out

Finally, let me come back to the key points ______ ❶ my talk. I told you that in the first quarter, more than half, or 52%, of eBay's revenues came ______ ❷ overseas. This is in line ______ ❸ the targets we set ______ ❹ in 2004 when we decided we wanted to continue to rely ______ ❺ overseas markets, especially China, to keep growing. Now what are our targets ______ ❻ the next few months? The first major step will be the introduction of our PayPal payment service ______ ❼ China. And then we will focus ______ ❽ finding customers in existing markets, such as the US and Germany.

## T3 Übersetzen Sie.

1. Lassen Sie mich die wichtigsten Ergebnisse zusammenfassen.
2. Ich würde jetzt gerne noch einmal die Hauptpunkte durchgehen.
3. Meiner Meinung nach müssen wir unsere Verkaufsstrategie ändern.
4. Mein Vorschlag ist, dass wir uns auf den deutschen Markt konzentrieren.
5. Ich komme jetzt zum Ende meiner Präsentation.
6. Jetzt lassen Sie uns das in die Tat umsetzen!

**T4 Finden Sie das fehlende Wort mithilfe der Erklärungen.**

1. What's the preposition? "Let me run … the main points again."
   ☐☐☐☐☐☐☐

2. The English word for *vorschlagen.*
   ☐☐☐☐☐☐☐

3. Another word for *target* – I'm sure we can reach this …
   ☐☐☐☐

4. The most important points or the … issues.
   ☐☐☐

5. Another verb for *summarize.*
   ☐☐☐☐☐

6. The opposite of *pros* (Vorteile).
   ☐☐☐☐

# 5 Fragen und Antworten

## 5.1 Konkrete Präsentationssituationen

### Fragen beantworten – die Rolle des Präsentierenden

**Sie haben die Frage nicht (richtig) verstanden**
Verwenden Sie einen der folgenden Sätze, um höflich nachzufragen, wenn Sie etwas nicht verstanden haben:

- I'm sorry. Could you repeat your question, please?
- I'm afraid I didn't quite catch that.
- I'm afraid I don't quite understand your question.

**Sie formulieren die Frage um**
Wenn die Frage lang oder kompliziert war, fassen Sie sie noch einmal in eigenen Worten zusammen:

- If I understood you correctly, you would like to know whether ...
- If I could just rephrase your question. You'd like to know if ...
- So, in other words you're asking if/how/when ...
- Let me just repeat your question. You are interested in ...

**Sie möchten die Frage nicht beantworten**
Wenn Sie eine Frage nicht beantworten möchten, erklären Sie das dem Fragesteller und liefern Sie, wenn möglich, eine höfliche Begründung:

- If you don't mind, I'd prefer not to discuss that today. Perhaps we can talk about that in our meeting next week.

- Perhaps we could deal with this at some other time. I'm afraid it would take too long to discuss this point now.
- I'm afraid that's not really what we're here to discuss today.

**Sie möchten die Frage später beantworten**

Bieten Sie an, die Frage später wieder aufzugreifen:

- Perhaps we could deal with this after the presentation?
- That's actually a point I wanted to discuss when we deal with ...
- If you don't mind, I'll come back to this question later.
- I'd prefer to answer this question in the course of my presentation.

**Sie wissen die Antwort nicht**

Wenn Sie die Antwort nicht wissen, verwenden Sie diese Formulierungen:

- Sorry, that's not my field.
- I'm afraid I don't know the answer to your question, but I'll try to find out for you.
- I'm afraid I'm not in a position to answer that.
- I don't know that off the top of my head. (auswendig)

Üblich ist dann, auf eine andere Person zu verweisen, die weiterhelfen kann.

- Perhaps Maria could help.
- But I'm sure Peter Bott from Sales could answer your question.

> ☞ **And by the way ...:** Vorsicht – Verwechslungsgefahr! Das englische Wort *branch* (Zweigstelle) hat nichts mit dem deutschen Wort Branche (*industry, line of business*) zu tun.

### Sie kommen nach einer Unterbrechung zum Thema zurück

Wenn Ihre Präsentation durch eine Frage unterbrochen wurde, fassen Sie die zuletzt besprochenen Punkte noch einmal zusammen:

- Before we go on, let me briefly summarize the points we've discussed.
- So, now I'd like to return to what we were discussing earlier.

## Fragen stellen – die Rolle des Teilnehmers

### Höflich unterbrechen

Wenn Sie während der Präsentation eine Frage stellen wollen, können Sie das mit den folgenden Formulierungen tun:

- Sorry to interrupt, but …
- Excuse me, …

Danach stellen Sie Ihre Frage, z.B.:

- Sorry to interrupt, but I'd like to know more about the details.
- Excuse me, may I ask how you arrived at these results?

### Direkte und indirekte Fragen

Verwenden Sie möglichst höfliche Frageformulierungen. Anstelle direkter Fragen, die mit einem Fragewort beginnen, verwenden Sie lieber indirekte Fragen. Indirekte und höfliche Fragen beginnen oft mit folgenden Formulierungen:

- Could/Can you tell me …
- Do you mind if I ask …
- Would you mind telling us …
- I'd like to know …

Vergleichen Sie die Beispiele:

| **Direkt** | **Indirekt** |
|---|---|
| When do you plan to move to Geneva? | Could you tell me when you plan to move to Geneva? |
| What is the project status? | Do you mind if I ask what the project status is? |
| Does it take more than two months to complete it? | Would you mind telling us if it takes more than two months to complete it? |

Beachten Sie, dass sich bei indirekten Fragen oft die Wortstellung im Satz verändert und Wörter wie *if* oder *whether* hinzugefügt werden müssen.

| **Direkte Frage** | **Indirekte Frage** |
|---|---|
| What's the current project status? | Can you tell me what the current project status is? |
| Is that the final decision? | Could you tell me whether/if that's the final decision? |

## 5.2 Präsentationsstrategien und interkulturelle Aspekte

**Vorbereitung auf Fragen der Teilnehmer**

Die Ansicht, man könne sich als Vortragende/-r auf Teilnehmerfragen nicht vorbereiten, ist weit verbreitet, aber zum Glück falsch. Wenn Sie sich in Ihrem Thema gut auskennen und sich gründlich auf Ihren Vortrag vorbereitet haben, gibt es hier keinen Grund zu Sorge und Nervosität.

> Überlegen Sie vor Ihrer Präsentation, welche Fragen auf Sie zukommen könnten, und erstellen Sie eine Liste.

Ganz allgemein kann man sagen, dass die meisten Fragen sich auf folgende Themenkomplexe beziehen, unabhängig vom Thema des Vortrags:

- Prozessablauf
- Zuständigkeit
- Kosten
- Fristen, Termine
- Zeitablauf
- Nutzen
- Alternativen
- Probleme, Risiken

Stellen Sie sicher, dass Sie alle Fragen auf Ihrer Liste zufriedenstellend beantworten können. Wenn möglich, üben Sie in einem Frage- und Antwortspiel mit einem Partner mögliche Antworten. Achten Sie auf Höflichkeit und verwenden Sie die entsprechenden englischen Redewendungen. Diese praktische Übung gibt Ihnen Sicherheit für Ihren Vortrag!

**Wenn Sie eine Antwort nicht wissen**

Auch bei gründlicher Vorbereitung bleibt natürlich ein Restrisiko und Sie können eine Frage einmal nicht beantworten. Das ist kein Beinbruch – Hauptsache, Sie sind auf diesen Fall vorbereitet und gehen offen damit um.

Überlegen Sie sich vor Ihrer Präsentation, wie Sie reagieren, wenn Sie einmal keine Antwort wissen.

Lernen Sie die entsprechenden englischen Redewendungen und üben Sie sie. Geben Sie ehrlich zu, dass Sie nicht antworten können. Versuchen Sie auf keinen Fall, spontan eine Antwort zu geben, die nicht fundiert ist. Das provoziert meist weitere Fragen, die Sie dann wahrscheinlich auch nicht beantworten können. Damit kann Ihre Kompetenz als Vortragende/-r infrage gestellt werden.
Wenn Sie dem Fragesteller keine (zufriedenstellende) Antwort geben können, bieten Sie Alternativen an.

- Versprechen Sie Klärung und spätere Beantwortung.
- Verweisen Sie auf einen kompetenten Ansprechpartner, der weiterhelfen kann.

**Umformulierung von Fragen**
Oft ist es empfehlenswert, dass der Vortragende Fragen anders formuliert und sie neu stellt. Das hat mehrere Vorteile:

- Alle Teilnehmer hören die Frage noch einmal.
- Missverständnisse können sofort geklärt werden.
- Aggressive Fragen können entschärft und positiver formuliert werden.

Wie aggressiv oder provozierend eine Frage klingt, hängt wesentlich von der Wortwahl ab. Einen positiven Ton erreichen Sie, indem Sie negative Wörter weglassen und neutrale Formulierungen verwenden. Vermeiden Sie möglichst Wörter wie *no, none, nothing, never* und Wörter, die an sich negativ besetzt sind, wie *disaster, to fail, loss, to mislead* etc.

> ☞ **And by the way ...:** Das Verb *to meet* bedeutet in einigen festen Ausdrücken *erfüllen* oder *einhalten: to meet a deadline* (einen Termin einhalten), *to meet requirements* (Anforderungen erfüllen).

Einige Beispiele:

| **Aggressive Frage** | **Neutrale Umformulierung** |
|---|---|
| Isn't there a cheaper solution? | You'd like to know what would be a cheaper solution. |
| Don't we have to cut costs? | You're asking whether we would have to cut costs. |

Ähnlich verfahren Sie mit provozierenden Fragen:

| **Provozierende Frage** | **Neutrale Umformulierung** |
|---|---|
| Do you honestly believe we can get the contract? | You're asking whether I think it is possible to get the contract. |
| Where on earth did you get these figures from? | If I understood you correctly, you'd like to know what the figures are based on. |

**Umgang mit Unterbrechungen durch Fragen**

Auch wenn Sie geplant haben, Fragen erst am Ende der Präsentation zu beantworten, kann es vorkommen, dass Zwischenfragen gestellt werden. Lassen Sie sich dadurch nicht aus dem Konzept bringen und reagieren Sie stets höflich, aber bestimmt.

Wenn es sich um eine Verständnisfrage handelt, sollten Sie sie kurz beantworten. Bei Fragen, die den Ablauf Ihrer Präsentation erheblich stören würden, verweisen Sie am besten höflich darauf, dass Sie sich später damit beschäftigen werden.

> Wenn Sie Fragen während der Präsentation beantworten, achten Sie darauf, dass Sie anschließend wieder den richtigen Einstieg in Ihr Thema finden.

Am besten wiederholen Sie kurz, was vor der Unterbrechung gesagt wurde. Fassen Sie die wichtigsten Punkte noch einmal schnell zusammen, damit alle Teilnehmer wieder im Boot sind.

**Fragen während oder am Ende der Präsentation?**
Beide Varianten haben Vor- und Nachteile. Ihre Entscheidung sollten Sie im Wesentlichen von zwei Kriterien abhängig machen:

- der Anzahl der Teilnehmer und
- der gewünschten Atmosphäre.

Vergleichen Sie die Vorzüge beider Methoden:

| Während des Vortrags | Am Ende des Vortrags |
|---|---|
| – Informell, seminarähnlich<br>– Teilnehmer sind stärker einbezogen<br>– Fragen können direkt geklärt werden | – Mehr Kontrolle über die Struktur<br>– Bessere Planung des zeitlichen Ablaufs<br>– Weniger Ablenkung |

Bei Präsentationen mit vielen Teilnehmern empfiehlt es sich, den Frageteil für den Schluss einzuplanen, da der Ablauf durch Zwischenfragen zu stark beeinträchtigt werden könnte.

**Angloamerikanische Verhaltensweisen im Frageteil**
Im angloamerikanischen Umfeld ist es üblich, dem oder der Vortragenden zunächst etwas Nettes zu sagen, bevor man eine Frage stellt. Das kann ein allgemeines Lob für die Präsentation oder die Bearbeitung des Themas sein oder eine Bemerkung darüber, dass ein bestimmter Teilaspekt besonders interessant war.

Auf jeden Fall wird durch eine positive Reaktion ein freundliches Klima zwischen Publikum und Vortragendem geschaffen.
Diese Methode wird auch angewendet, wenn ein Fragesteller Kritik äußern möchte. Fallen Sie nicht mit der Tür ins Haus, sondern mildern Sie Ihre Bemerkung durch eine höfliche Einleitung ab.

**Tipps für den Frageteil**

1. Achten Sie genau auf die gestellte Frage.
2. Stellen Sie sicher, dass Sie sie richtig verstanden haben.
3. Formulieren Sie die Frage mit eigenen Worten.
4. Wenn Sie die Frage erst später beantworten wollen, sagen Sie das und begründen Sie es.
5. Falls Sie die Antwort nicht wissen, geben Sie das zu und bieten Sie Klärung an.
6. Beantworten Sie unpassende Fragen so kurz wie möglich.
7. Stellen Sie sicher, dass der Fragesteller mit Ihrer Antwort zufrieden ist.

## 5.3 Vokabeln und Redewendungen auf einen Blick

**Den Frageteil einleiten**

- Are there any questions?
- And now I'll be happy to answer any questions you may have.

**Fragen klären und umformulieren**

- I'm afraid I didn't (quite) catch that.
- I'm sorry, could you repeat your question, please?
- So, if I understood you correctly, you would like to know whether …
- So, in other words you are asking whether …
- If I could just rephrase your question. You'd like to know …
- Does that answer your question?

**Eine Antwort umgehen**

- If you don't mind, could we discuss that on another occasion?
- I'm afraid that's not really what we're discussing today.
- Well, actually I'd prefer not to discuss that today.

**Zugeben, dass man etwas nicht weiß**

- Sorry, I don't know that off the top of my head.
- I'm afraid I'm not in a position to answer that question at the moment.
- I'm afraid I don't know the answer to your question, but I'll try to find out for you.
- Sorry, that's not my field. But I'm sure Peter Bott from Sales could answer your question.

**Fragen auf später verschieben**

- If you don't mind, I'll deal with / come back to this point later in my presentation.
- Can we get back to this point a bit later?
- I'd prefer to answer your question in the course of my presentation.
- Would you mind waiting until the question and answer session at the end?
- Perhaps we could go over this after the presentation.

**Nach Unterbrechungen zusammenfassen**

- Before we go on, let me briefly summarize the points we've discussed.
- So, now I'd like to return to what we were discussing earlier.
- Let me just go back to the story I told you earlier.
- Remember, …
- Well, perhaps you remember what I said at the beginning of my talk …

**Fragen stellen**

- Sorry to interrupt, but I'd like to know …
- Excuse me, may I ask a question?
- Could you tell us/me …
- Do you mind if I ask whether/what/when/how …
- Would you mind telling us/me …

## 5.4 Übungen

**Ü1 Setzen Sie die passenden Ausdrücke ein.**

Could you give us – Does that mean – Are there any questions – Go ahead – Excuse me – No, not at all – May I ask – I suggest you speak to – I'd be interested – Would you mind

*Presenter* ________________ (1) ?

*Susanne* Yes, I have a question. ________________ (2) some background information on Track Ltd?

*Presenter* Certainly. They're one of the leading manufacturers of outdoor equipment in the UK with more than 35 factories worldwide.

*Tim* ________________ (3) telling us why you've chosen them as partners?

*Presenter* ________________ (4). The answer's quite simple. We were very impressed with the quality of their products and their prices are very attractive.

*Annette* ________________ (5) a question?

*Presenter* Yes, of course. ________________ (6).

*Annette* ________________ (7) to know what their terms of payment are.

*Presenter* I'm afraid I can't answer that question. ________________ (8) Sylvia Becker – she would be the right person to ask.

| | |
|---|---|
| *Alex* | _______________ 9. You mentioned a German office. _______________ 10 we do business through them? |
| *Presenter* | That's right. We need to discuss the details though. |

**Ü2 Fügen Sie die Satzteile richtig zusammen.**

| | | |
|---|---|---|
| 1. And now I'll be happy | a understand your question. | ☐ |
| 2. What exactly do | b another question | ☐ |
| 3. Are there | c to answer any questions. | ☐ |
| 4. I'm afraid I don't quite | d I'd prefer not to discuss that today | ☐ |
| 5. Could you be | e you mean by that? | ☐ |
| 6. I have | f how they will be organized? | ☐ |
| 7. If you don't mind, | g a bit more specific? | ☐ |
| 8. Mr Menzel, you | h not my field. | ☐ |
| 9. Could you tell us | i any more questions? | ☐ |
| 10. Sorry, that's | j have a question? | ☐ |

**Ü3 Wandeln Sie die direkten Fragen in höfliche Fragen um.**

1. Are there any other options?
~ *May I ask* if there are any other options?

2. What would that mean for us?
~ *Do you mind telling me* what that would mean for us?

3. How do we compare with other firms?
*May I ask* ______________________________
______________________________

4. Will we cooperate with our branches in the UK?
*Can you tell me* ______________________________
______________________________

5. How did you arrive at these results?
*Would you mind telling me* ______________________________
______________________________

6. Are there any figures to back this up?
*Could you tell me* ______________________________
______________________________

**Ü4 Ordnen Sie die Fragen aus der vorherigen Übung diesen Antworten zu.**

a Very well. At the moment we are market leader.

b Yes. As I said earlier, I'll be passing out handouts with the latest data.

c Yes, we will. I've already contacted the London office.

d Well, first of all, more work for each of us.

e Of course. Basically we have two alternatives.

f Not at all. They are based on the latest study.

## Ü5 Setzen Sie die passenden Wörter ein.

answer – mean – specific – understand – mentioned – mind

1. You were talking about software problems. What exactly do you ______________ by that?
2. Well, I ______________earlier that the new software is being tested at the moment. (...) Does that ____________ your question?
3. Would you______________ telling us whether the new software will help to improve our company's image?
4. I'm afraid I don't quite ________________ your question. Could you be a bit more ____________?

## Ü6 Fügen Sie die Satzteile richtig zusammen.

| | | |
|---|---|---|
| 1. Good point, but I'd prefer | a your question please? | ☐ |
| 2. Perhaps we could | b deal with this at some other time. | ☐ |
| 3. Could you repeat | c off the top of my head. | ☐ |
| 4. I'm afraid that's | d not to discuss that today. | ☐ |
| 5. I'm sure Ms Maier | e answer your question? | ☐ |
| 6. Sorry, I don't | f not my field. | ☐ |
| 7. I'm afraid I don't know that | g could answer that question for you. | ☐ |
| 8. I'm afraid I'm not | h in a position to comment on that. | ☐ |
| 9. Does that | i quite understand your question. | ☐ |

**Ü7 Setzen Sie die passenden Wörter ein. Manchmal ist mehr als eine Lösung möglich.**

answer – deal – go – mention – mind – move – prefer – recap – summarize

1. Well, actually, I'd ____________ to answer your question after the presentation.

2. To ____________ what we were discussing, let me ____________ the following points.

3. Sorry, but I'd rather not ____________ with this question now as we'll be looking at that in detail later on this morning.

4. Let me just ____________ back to what we were discussing earlier.

5. I'll ____________ this question in the course of my presentation.

6. Before we ____________ on, let me briefly ____________ the main points we have been talking about.

7. I'm sorry, but would you ____________ waiting until the question period?

# Fit for Presenting in English? Test Yourself!

**T1 Setzen Sie die passenden Ausdrücke ein.**

my field – could you tell us – don't mind – return to – could answer – question – actually – regarding

1. I have a ______________________. It's about the piloting stage. Which division will start piloting the software first?

2. If you ________________________, I'd prefer not to discuss that today.

3. ________________________, there will be a meeting next week where that will be decided. OK? ...

4. You spoke about special training courses earlier. ________________________ how they will be organized?

5. Sorry, I'm afraid that's not ______________. But I'm sure Linda Koll from the training department ________________________ that question.

6. Now I'd like to ____________________ what we were discussing earlier.

7. Excuse me, I have a question ___________________ pricing.

**T2 Worum geht es in den Dialogen A–C? Ordnen Sie die Themenkomplexe den Gesprächen zu.**

a keine Antwort wissen
b Frage umformulieren
c Frage auf später verschieben
d auf jemand anderen verweisen
e unbekannten Begriff erklären

**A** ☐

| | |
|---|---|
| *Presenter* | The main advantages of ‚smart' credit cards are … |
| *Man* | Sorry to interrupt, but could you explain what ‚smart' means in this context? |
| *Presenter* | Yes, sure. It means that big credit card companies like Visa and Mastercard use special microchips instead of the usual magnetic strips on their cards. Does that answer your question? |
| *Man* | Yes, thank you, Peter. |
| *Presenter* | OK, so let's go back to the main advantages of ‚smart' credit cards. … |

**B** ☐

| | |
|---|---|
| *Presenter* | And talking of mergers, don't forget the successful German haircare company, Wella, which was taken over by Procter and Gamble only a few years ago. What we need to discuss is whether it's the right moment for us to consider a merger with Carter Financial Services. |
| *Woman* | Could you tell us what their turnover was last year? |

| | |
|---|---|
| *Presenter* | Sorry, if you don't mind, I'd like to answer your question a bit later when we discuss the financial side of this merger. OK, I was just moving on to the timing of the merger and … |

**c** ☐

| | |
|---|---|
| *Presenter* | So, delivery of the units has been set for 15 May. That gives us three months to handle the production and packaging. I'd like to turn now to the … |
| *Woman* | Ah, excuse me. Do you really think that's realistic? I mean, three months. What about our staff problems? |
| *Presenter* | If I have understood you correctly, Louise, your question is how we can meet the delivery date as we are slightly understaffed in production at the moment. Well, let me answer your question right away. First of all … |

## T3 Übersetzen Sie.

1. Wenn ich Sie richtig verstehe, möchten Sie wissen, wie das System funktioniert.
2. Diese Frage kann ich leider nicht beantworten.
3. Vielleicht können wir diesen Punkt bei anderer Gelegenheit besprechen.
4. Mich würde interessieren, ob wir den Termin einhalten können.
5. Darf ich Sie fragen, wie Sie zu diesen Zahlen gekommen sind?
6. Ich schlage vor, Sie sprechen mit Frau Sauer aus der Marketingabteilung.

## Checkliste für englischsprachige Präsentationen

### A Vorbereitung auf inhaltliche Aspekte der Präsentation

Zweck/Ziel der Präsentation: informieren ☐ verkaufen ☐ schulen ☐ überzeugen ☐

Thema der Präsentation: ____________

3 Hauptpunkte: 1 ________ 2 ________ 3 ________

Was sollen die Zuhörer am Ende der Präsentation wissen/können? ________

**Visualisierung**

Wie viele Folien, Grafiken etc. werde ich einsetzen? ________

Unterstützen sie meine Aussagen? ________

Sind sie klar gestaltet und einfach zu verstehen? ________

Sind sie gut lesbar? ________

Haben sie aussagekräftige Überschriften? ________

Haben sie möglichst wenig Text (*rule of six*)? ________

### B Feedback: Nachbereitung der Präsentation

#### 1 Sprache und Kommunikation

Wie gut habe ich meine Nervosität bewältigt? ________

Wie war meine Körpersprache? ________

Konnten die Teilnehmer mich verstehen? ja, immer ☐ ↘ meistens ☐ ↘ oft nicht ☐

Hatte ich Probleme, mich in englischer Sprache auszudrücken? ja, ständig ☐ ↘ ja, oft ☐ ↘ ja, manchmal ☐ ↘ nein ☐

Welche Wörter oder Redewendungen haben mir gefehlt? ________

#### 2 Organisation meiner Präsentation

Hatte die Präsentation die richtige Länge? zu lang ☐ zu kurz ☐ genau richtig ☐

War genug Zeit, um Fragen zu beantworten? ja ☐ ↘ nein ☐

## 3 Inhalt und Ablauf der Präsentation

| ***a Einleitung*** | |
|---|---|
| Habe ich den Zweck meiner Präsentation erklärt? | ja ☐ ↘ nein ☐ |
| Habe ich die Struktur erläutert? | ja ☐ ↘ nein ☐ |
| Habe ich deutlich gemacht, für wen die Präsentation relevant ist? | ja ☐ ↘ nein ☐ |
| Wie kann ich meine Einleitung verbessern? ______________________ | |

| ***b Hauptteil*** | |
|---|---|
| Habe ich meine Argumente/ Punkte deutlich gemacht? | ja ☐ ↘ nein ☐ |
| Habe ich *Signposting* effektiv genutzt? | ja ☐ ↘ nein ☐ |
| Habe ich wichtige Punkte besonders betont? | ja ☐ ↘ nein ☐ |
| Habe ich wichtige Punkte jeweils zusammengefasst? | ja ☐ ↘ nein ☐ |
| Habe ich Visualisierungsmittel gut eingesetzt? | ja ☐ ↘ nein ☐ |
| Wie kann ich den Hauptteil verbessern? ______________________ | |

| ***c Schlussteil*** | |
|---|---|
| Habe ich die wichtigsten Punkte zusammengefasst? | ja ☐ ↘ nein ☐ |
| Habe ich die Teilnehmer zum Handeln aufgefordert? | ja ☐ ↘ nein ☐ |
| Habe ich beim Publikum einen starken Eindruck hinterlassen? | ja ☐ ↘ nein ☐ |
| Wie kann ich den Schlussteil verbessern? ______________________ | |

| ***d Frage- und Antwortteil*** | |
|---|---|
| Wie gut konnte ich mit Fragen umgehen? | sehr gut ☐ nicht sehr gut ☐ gar nicht gut ☐ |
| Welche Fragen hatte ich nicht erwartet? ______________________ | |
| Wie kann ich in Zukunft mit Fragen besser umgehen? ______________ | |

# Lösungen

## Kapitel 1

### Seite 22/23

**Ü1**

1. First of all; thank
2. glad
3. introduce
4. present
5. particularly
6. happy; make; notice
7. screen; topic
8. important; involved

**Ü2**

2 … give e
3 … talking c
4 … bring b
5 … report h
6 … update a
7 … looking g
8 … begin f

### Seite 24/25

**Ü3**

1. I'm aware that
2. to come here
3. As you probably
4. I'm the new
5. I'd like to present
6. concept for
7. Today's topic
8. I'll need your help

**Ü4**

1. You know; came across; magazines
2. Imagine; responsible; go about it
3. Did you know
4. asking you; tell you why

**Ü5**

1. f
2. a
3. c
4. e
5. h
6. g
7. d
8. b

### Seite 26/27

**Ü6**

1. for
2. into
3. of
4. at
5. on
6. with
7. about
8. to
9. during

**Ü7**

1. c
2. d
3. h
4. g
5. i
6. f
7. a
8. e
9. b

### Seite 28/29

**T1**

1. g
2. c
3. b
4. d

| | | | |
|---|---|---|---|
| 5. a | 6. f | 7. e | 8. h |

**T2**

1. Did you know that AA saved $ 40,000 by eliminating one olive from each salad served in first class?
2. I read in an article that overweight in the US is far more dangerous than terrorism. I tend to agree with that!
3. Imagine you won a million euros. Who would you tell first?
4. Can we really compete with the Chinese? Of course we can!

**T3**

1. OK, let's get started.
2. The topic/subject of my presentation today is customer satisfaction.
3. My presentation/talk will take/last about 30 minutes.
4. I will be concentrating on three points.
5. First of all, we'll have a look at the current project status.
6. Did you know that this car is very popular in China?

### Seite 30/31

**T4**

| | | | |
|---|---|---|---|
| 1. start | 3. Finally | 5. all | 7. areas |
| 2. Then | 4. divided | 6. After | 8. third |

**T5**

| | | |
|---|---|---|
| 1. begin | 3. I'm | 5. responsible for |
| 2. sections | 4. after that; turn | 6. I realize |

## Kapitel 2

### Seite 45

**Ü1**

| | |
|---|---|
| 1. a look | 2. on the board |
| 3. have a | 4. next slide; illustration |
| 5. can see | 6. go back; page; just flip |

### Seite 46/47

**Ü2**

| | | |
|---|---|---|
| 1. e | 3. a | 5. d |
| 2. c | 4. f | 6. b |

**Ü3**

| | | | |
|---|---|---|---|
| 1. look at | 2. explain | 3. colours | 4. indicate |

5. left-hand 6. line 7. attention 8. blue

**Ü4**

1. divided
2. shown
3. see
4. total
5. surprised
6. amount
7. account

**Ü5**

1. just over/about 90,000
2. almost / just under / nearly / about 15 %
3. almost / nearly / just under €2m
4. just over / roughly / approximately 18 degrees
5. about / just under / almost 400 m²

## Seite 48/49

**Ü6**

1. Telephone costs have risen since January.
2. Sales dropped at the beginning of the year.
3. Income tax has increased over the past 30 years.
4. Gas prices went up last month.
5. The number of customers has grown since 2004.
6. Surprisingly, interest rates fell yesterday.

**Ü7**

2. ... fell dramatically
3. ... have declined gradually
4. ... rose sharply
5. ... has grown considerably
6. ... has decreased steadily

**Ü8**

1. b
2. d
3. f
4. c
5. a
6. e

## Seite 50/51

**Ü9**

1. fluctuated
2. rose
3. decline
4. slumped
5. picking up
6. reached

**Ü10**

1. decrease, go down, fall
2. reach a high
3. stay the same, remain stable
4. go down, decrease, fall, drop
5. get worse, deteriorate
6. increase, rise, go up

**T1**

| | |
|---|---|
| 1. slide | 3. look; this chart; shows |
| 2. see; segment | 4. bar; left |

**T2**

| | | |
|---|---|---|
| 1. in; until | 4. until | 7. around |
| 2. between | 5. from | 8. by |
| 3. to | 6. of | 9. at |

## Seite 52/53

**T3**

| | | |
|---|---|---|
| 1. richtig | 3. falsch, raise | 5. falsch, rise |
| 2. falsch, rose | 4. richtig | 6. falsch, raised |

**T4**

1. Let's have a closer look at this table. Let's look at this table more closely.
2. On the next slide you will see the sales figures for the first quarter.
3. This pie chart shows our market share in per cent.
4. I'd like to draw/call your attention to the following facts.
5. According to the study travel expenses have increased / risen / gone up sharply since the year 2000.
6. Our productivity reached a low in December.

**T5**

| | | |
|---|---|---|
| 1. fell | 3. plunged | 5. have doubled |
| 2. has improved | 4. has grown | 6. slumped |

# Kapitel 3

## Seite 68/69

**Ü1**

1. As I said earlier, I'll be focussing on our new sales strategies.
2. This brings us directly to my next question.
3. This leads to the next point, which is price.
4. Let's now turn to the issue of customer service.
5. As I mentioned before, I'd like to give you a brief overview of our activities.
6. I'd like to come back to this question later.
7. Let's go back to what we were discussing earlier.

8. Before I move on to my next point, let me go through the main issues once more.

**Ü2**

1. with regard
2. Moreover
3. concerns
4. Apart from
5. regarding
6. According to

**Ü3**

1. g
2. f
3. d
4. e
5. c
6. h
7. a
8. b

## Seite 70/71

**Ü4**

2. As you already know, Tony Dale is our new marketing manager for print media.
3. As I said at the beginning of my talk, we can't operate from our local airport because we have no permission.
4. As I explained ten minutes ago, we have to choose between two options.
5. As you can see on this slide, sales have increased by 10% since the beginning of the year.

**Ü5**

1. extremely dangerous
2. absolutely necessary
3. highly interesting
4. surprisingly good
5. completely useless
6. absolutely safe
7. incredibly cheap

**Ü6**

1. draw your attention
2. you will see
3. The figures also show that
4. It's quite remarkable
5. On the other hand
6. can we explain
7. have a look
8. let's talk about

## Seite 72/73

**Ü7**

1. are (currently) having
2. identify
3. deal
4. cope
5. prevent
6. accept
7. don't solve
8. will ('ll) run

**Ü8**

1. e
2. g
3. b
4. a
5. c
6. d
7. h
8. f

**T1**

1. main points
2. discussing
3. inform
4. sum up
5. covered
6. wanted
7. leads
8. back

## Seite 74/75

**T2**

1. deal
2. cope
3. identify
4. take care
5. solve
6. clarify

**T3**

1. Let's now move on to the next point/issue.
2. Despite software problems we were able to achieve a surprisingly good result.
3. The reason for this decline/slump is the poor economic situation. / The decline/slump is/was caused by the poor economic situation.
4. I'd like to point out / emphasize / stress the importance of this change / how important this change is.
5. As I mentioned before/earlier, I'll first give you a brief overview.
6. On the other hand, we have to deal with the consequences.

**T4**

1. however
2. Although
3. Whereas
4. Despite
5. Consequently
6. On the other hand

# Kapitel 4

## Seite 86/87

**Ü1**

1. briefly summarize
2. figures we have
3. now approaching
4. to highlight
5. final point
6. my opinion
7. come back
8. suggest that

### Ü2

1. Clearly
2. never
3. strategy
4. dramatic
5. production
6. I

### Ü3

1. on
2. In
3. to
4. for
5. through
6. out
7. about
8. by

## Seite 88/89

### Ü4

1. story; Remember
2. convinced that; want to miss
3. key question
4. briefly recap

### Ü5

1. Well, that brings me to the end of my talk today.
2. Before I stop, let me go over the key issues again.
3. As a final point, let me say what this means for us.
4. Finally, I'd like to highlight one key issue.
5. To sum up then, we first looked at the new product range.
6. That covers just about everything I wanted to say about logistics.

### Ü6

1. f
2. b
3. e
4. g
5. c
6. a
7. d

## Seite 90/91

### T1

1. b
2. c
3. d
4. c
5. b
6. a
7. d
8. c

### T2

1. of
2. from
3. with
4. out
5. on
6. for
7. in
8. on

### T3

1. Let me summarize / sum up / recap the most important results.

2. I'd now like to go over the main points again.
3. In my opinion we need / have to change our sales strategy.
4. I suggest that we concentrate on the German market.
5. I'm now approaching/nearing the end of my presentation/ talk.
6. Let's now put it into practice!

### Seite 92

**T4**

| | | |
|---|---|---|
| 1. through | 3. goal | 5. recap |
| 2. suggest | 4. key | 6. cons |

## Kapitel 5

### Seite 104/105

**Ü1**

| | |
|---|---|
| 1. Are there any questions | 6. Go ahead. |
| 2. Could you give us | 7. I'd be interested |
| 3. Would you mind | 8. I suggest you speak to |
| 4. No, not at all | 9. Excuse me |
| 5. May I ask | 10. Does that mean |

**Ü2**

| | | | | |
|---|---|---|---|---|
| 1. c | 3. i | 5. g | 7. d | 9. f |
| 2. e | 4. a | 6. b | 8. j | 10. h |

### Seite 106/107

**Ü3**

3. May I ask how we compare with other firms?
4. Can you tell me if/whether we'll cooperate with our branches in the UK?
5. Would you mind telling me how you arrived at these results?
6. Could you tell me if/whether there are any figures to back this up?

### Ü4

1. e
2. d
3. a
4. c
5. f
6. b

### Ü5

1. mean
2. mentioned; answer
3. mind
4. understand; specific

### Ü6

1. d
2. b
3. a
4. f
5. g
6. i
7. c
8. h
9. e

## Seite 108/109

### Ü7

1. prefer
2. summarize/ recap; mention
3. deal
4. go
5. answer
6. move; summarize/recap
7. mind

### T1

1. question
2. don't mind
3. Actually
4. Could you tell us
5. my field; could answer
6. return to
7. regarding

## Seite 110/111

### T2

A e

B c

C b

### T3

1. If I understood you correctly, you would like to know how the system works.
2. I'm afraid I can't answer that question.
3. Perhaps we can get back to that point later. / Perhaps we could discuss that on another occasion.
4. I'd be interested to know if we can meet the deadline.
5. May I ask how you arrived at these figures?
6. I suggest you speak to Ms Sauer from the marketing department.

## Alphabetischer Wortschatz Englisch – Deutsch

| | |
|---|---|
| **according to** | laut, nach |
| **to account for** | betragen, sich belaufen auf |
| **to achieve** | erreichen |
| **additionally** | zusätzlich |
| **aim** | Ziel |
| **amount** | Betrag |
| **annual** | jährlich |
| to **appreciate** | zu schätzen wissen |
| to **approach** | sich nähern |
| **approximately** | etwa, ungefähr |
| **around** | ungefähr, etwa |
| to **attend** | teilnehmen (an) |
| to **average** | durchschnittlich erreichen |
| | |
| **bar chart** | Säulendiagramm |
| **based on** | basierend auf |
| **board** | Tafel |
| **branch** | Niederlassung, Zweigstelle |
| **breakdown** | Aufteilung, Aufschlüsselung |
| | |
| to **clarify** | klären |
| **column** | Spalte |
| to **compare with** | dastehen im Vergleich mit |
| **compared to** | verglichen mit |
| **competitor** | Konkurrent/-in, Mitbewerber/-in |
| to **complain** | sich beschweren |
| **concerning** | betreffend |
| **conclude,** to ~ | abschließen, zum Ende kommen |
| **consequence** | Folge, Konsequenz |
| **consequently** | dementsprechend, infolgedessen |
| **considerable** | beträchtlich |
| to **cope with** | fertig werden mit |
| to **crash** | abstürzen |
| **current status** | aktueller Stand |
| | |
| **data projector** | Beamer |
| to **deal with** | sich befassen mit |
| to **decline** | sinken, zurückgehen, abnehmen |
| to **decrease** | abnehmen, fallen |
| **delay** | Verspätung, Verzögerung |

| | |
|---|---|
| to **describe** | beschreiben |
| to **deteriorate** | sich verschlechtern |
| **development** | Entwicklung |
| **diagram** | Strukturbild, Diagramm |
| **disappointed** | enttäuscht |
| **divided** | aufgeteilt |
| **dividend** | Dividende |
| **division** | Sparte, Abteilung |
| to **draw s.o.'s attention to** | Aufmerksamkeit lenken auf |
| to **drop** | fallen |
| | |
| **effort** | Anstrengung |
| to **emphasize** | betonen, hervorheben |
| **employee** | Angestellte/-r |
| **equipment** | Ausstattung, Geräte |
| to **evaluate** | bewerten, einstufen |
| | |
| to **feel free to do sth** | etwas ohne zu zögern tun |
| **figures** | Zahlen |
| **flip chart** | Flipchart |
| **flowchart** | Flussdiagramm |
| to **fluctuate** | schwanken |
| | |
| to **go up** | steigen |
| **goal** | Ziel |
| **graph** | Kurve |
| | |
| to **handle** | bewältigen, bearbeiten |
| to **highlight** | hervorheben |
| to **hit a low** | einen Tiefpunkt erreichen |
| | |
| to **improve** | (sich) verbessern |
| **in addition to** | zusätzlich, darüber hinaus |
| **in charge of,** to **be ~** | verantwortlich sein für |
| **in connection with** | im Zusammenhang mit |
| to **increase** | steigen, steigern |
| to **interrupt** | unterbrechen, ins Wort fallen |
| to **introduce (oneself)** | (sich) vorstellen |
| **involved in,** to **be ~** | beteiligt sein an |
| **issue** | aktuelle Frage, Thema |
| | |
| **joint venture** | Gemeinschaftsunternehmen |

| | |
|---|---|
| **key points** | Hauptpunkte |
| **key questions** | Schlüsselfragen |
| to **last** | dauern |
| to **lead to** | führen zu |
| **(line) graph** | Kurvendiagramm |
| **main part** | Hauptteil |
| **major** | Haupt-, wichtig |
| **map** | Karte |
| to **mention** | erwähnen |
| **moderate(ly)** | mäßig, gemäßigt |
| to **move on** | fortfahren, weitergehen |
| **nearly** | fast |
| to **notice** | (be)merken |
| **objective** | Zielsetzung, Zweck |
| **option** | Möglichkeit |
| **organizational chart** | Organigramm |
| **output** | Ausstoß, Menge |
| **overseas** | Ausland, Übersee |
| **overview** | Überblick, Übersicht |
| to **pass on** | weiterreichen |
| **permission** | Erlaubnis, Genehmigung |
| to **pick up** | *hier:* zunehmen |
| **pie chart** | Tortendiagramm |
| **plant** | Werk, Betrieb(sanlage) |
| to **plummet** | abstürzen |
| to **plunge** | abstürzen, absacken |
| **policy** | Geschäfts-, Firmenpolitik |
| **prescription drugs** | rezeptpflichtige Arzneimittel |
| to **present** | präsentieren |
| **previous** | vorhergehend |
| **probably** | wahrscheinlich |
| **procedure** | Verfahren |
| **product range** | Produktpalette |
| to **prompt** | auslösen, veranlassen |
| to **propose** | vorschlagen |
| **pros and cons** | Für und Wider |
| **purpose** | Zweck, Absicht |

| | |
|---|---|
| **quarter** | Quartal |
| **question and answer session** | Fragerunde |
| to **quote** | zitieren |
| | |
| to **raise sth** | etwas erhöhen |
| to **reach a high** | einen Höchststand erreichen |
| to **recap** | (kurz) zusammenfassen |
| to **recommend** | empfehlen |
| **record high** | Rekordhöhe, Höchststand |
| to **recover** | sich erholen |
| to **reduce** | senken, verringern |
| **regarding** | betreffend |
| to **rely on sth** | sich auf etwas stützen, verlassen |
| to **remain** | (ver)bleiben |
| to **remain stable** | stabil bleiben |
| to **report on** | berichten über |
| to **result in** | führen zu |
| **revenue** | Einkünfte, Einahmen |
| to **review** | zusammenfassen; überdenken |
| to **rise** | (auf)steigen |
| to **rocket** | in die Höhe schießen |
| **roughly** | ungefähr, etwa |
| to **run through** | durchgehen, überfliegen |
| | |
| **sales force** | Verkaufspersonal |
| **schedule, tight ~** | enger Zeitplan |
| **screen** | Bildschirm, Leinwand |
| **sharp** | heftig |
| to **shoot up** | in die Höhe schnellen |
| to **shrink** | schrumpfen |
| **significantly** | deutlich |
| **slide** | Präsentationsfolie |
| **slightly** | geringfügig |
| **slump** | Absturz, Rückgang |
| to **slump** | sinken, stürzen |
| to **soar** | in die Höhe schnellen |
| to **solve** | lösen |
| **steadily** | stetig |
| **subject** | Thema |
| **suggestion** | Vorschlag |
| to **sum up** | zusammenfassen |
| to **summarize** | zusammenfassen |

| | |
|---|---|
| **supply problems** | Lieferschwierigkeiten |
| **support** | Unterstützung |
| **survey** | Untersuchung |
| | |
| **table** | Tabelle, Tafel |
| to **tackle** | anpacken, in Angriff nehmen |
| to **take care of** | sich kümmern um |
| **target** | Ziel, Zielvorgabe |
| **technical drawing** | technische Zeichnung |
| **temporary staff** | Zeitpersonal |
| to **tend to** | neigen zu, tendieren zu |
| **terms of payment** | Zahlungsbedingungen |
| **thus** | somit, folglich |
| **topic** | Thema |
| **transparency** | Folie |
| **turnover** | Umsatz |
| | |
| **understaffed** | unterbesetzt |
| **unemployment** | Arbeitslosigkeit |
| | |
| **venture** | Versuch, Unternehmung |
| | |
| to **weigh** | abwägen |
| **whiteboard** | Kunststofftafel |
| **with reference to** | in Bezug auf |
| **with regard to** | in Bezug auf |
| **with respect to** | hinsichtlich |

## Über die Autorin

Marion Grussendorf ist seit mehr als 15 Jahren Trainerin für Business English in Wirtschaft und Industrie.
Sie ist Geschäftsführerin der ACADIA Medien und Kommunikation GmbH in Köln und leitet u.a. Schulungen und Workshops im Bereich Wirtschaftsenglisch in internationalen Unternehmen.
Seit einigen Jahren arbeitet sie außerdem als freie Autorin und Beraterin für den Cornelsen Verlag und hat mehrere Bücher verfasst, die sich mit den Themen Telefonieren und Präsentieren in englischer Sprache beschäftigen.